Oxford Bibliographical Society
Publications

NEW SERIES VOLUME XIV

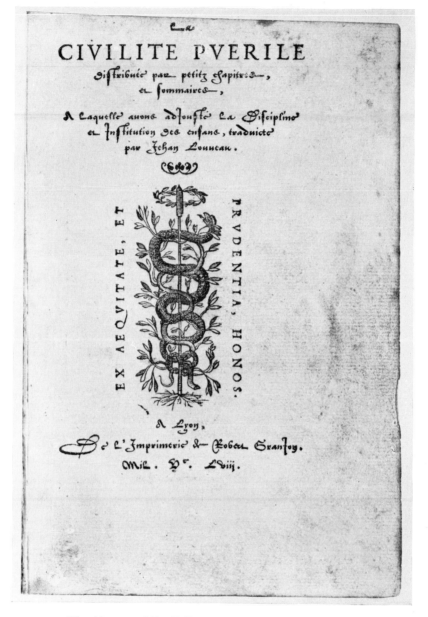

CIVILITE PVERILE

distribuée par petitz chapitres,
et sommaires,

A laquelle auons adiousté la Discipline
et Institution des enfans, traduicte
par Jehan Louueau.

EX AEQVITATE, ET PRVDENTIA, HONOS.

A Lyon,
De L'Imprimerie de Robert Granjon.
Mil. D. LViij.

The title-page of *La Civilite puerile*, Lyons, R. Granjon, 1558

CIVILITÉ TYPES

BY

HARRY CARTER

AND

H. D. L. VERVLIET

Published for

THE OXFORD BIBLIOGRAPHICAL SOCIETY

by the OXFORD UNIVERSITY PRESS

1966

Inquiries about the Society and its publications
should be addressed to the Hon. Secretary, Oxford Bibliographical Society
c/o Bodleian Library, Oxford

©   *H. G. Carter and H. D. L. Vervliet*

PRINTED IN GREAT BRITAIN

ACKNOWLEDGEMENTS

WE have been aided in our search for books set in Civilité types by many friends and colleagues, and we are very grateful for their kindness. Our special thanks are due to the librarians at the Bibliothèque Nationale at Paris, the University Libraries at Ghent and Geneva, the City Library at Antwerp, and the Royal Libraries at The Hague and Brussels. Professor H. de la Fontaine Verwey of Amsterdam, Dr. E. Braches of Haarlem, Mme Veyrin-Forrer and M. L. Scheler at Paris, Mr. Mike Parker in New York, and Mr. Colin Clair in London generously passed on to us some of the fruits of their own researches.

We are greatly indebted to the Curator of the Museum Plantin-Moretus, to Messrs. Joh. Enschedé en Zonen, and to Messrs. Deberny-Peignot for their generosity in supplying illustrations.

To those members of the Oxford Bibliographical Society who were good enough to read the book in manuscript and give us advice on parts of it within their special competence we are also very grateful.

H. C.
H. D. L. V.

CONTENTS

LIST OF ILLUSTRATIONS

ABBREVIATIONS USED IN REFERENCES

Amsterdam: Amsterdam, Universiteitsbibliotheek.

Antwerp: Antwerp, Stadsbibliotheek.

Antwerp, Ruusbroec: Antwerp, Bibliotheek van het Ruusbroec-Genootschap.

Baudrier: H. and L. Baudrier, *Bibliographie lyonnaise* (Lyons and Paris, 1895–1912).

BB: *Bibliotheca Belgica: bibliographie générale des Pays-Bas* (Ghent, 1880–   ).

Berry and Johnson: W. T. Berry and A. F. Johnson, *Catalogue of Specimens of Printing Types by English and Scottish Printers and Founders* (1934).

BM: London, British Museum.

BN: Paris, Bibliothèque Nationale.

Bodl.: Oxford, Bodleian Library.

Brussels: Brussels, Bibliothèque Royale.

Cartier: A. Cartier, *Bibliographie des éditions des De Tournes* (Paris, 1937).

Edinburgh: Edinburgh, National Library of Scotland.

Enschedé, *Fonderies*: C. Enschedé, *Fonderies de caractères et leur matériel dans les Pays-Bas du XVe au XIXe siècle* (Haarlem, 1908).

Early Inv.: M. Parker, K. Melis, and H. D. L. Vervliet, 'Early Inventories of Punches, Matrices, and Moulds in the Plantin-Moretus Archives', *De Gulden Passer*, 38 (Antwerp, 1960), pp. 1–139.

Freiburg i. Br.: Freiburg im Breisgau, Universitätsbibliothek.

Geneva: Geneva, Bibliothèque publique et universitaire.

Ghent: Ghent, Universiteitsbibliotheek.

Haarlem, Enschedé: Haarlem, Stichting Museum Enschedé.

Laceulle-van de Kerk: H. J. Laceulle-van de Kerk, *De Haarlemse Drukkers en Boekverkoopers van 1540 tot 1600* (The Hague, 1951).

Leyden: Leyden, Universiteitsbibliotheek.

Liège: Liège, Bibliothèque de l'Université.

London, St. Bride: London, St. Bride Institute Printing Library.

Louvain: Louvain, Bibliothèque de l'Université.

Lyons: Lyons, Bibliothèque de la Ville de Lyon.

Moes–Burger: E. W. Moes and C. F. Burger, *De Amsterdamsche Boekdrukkers en Uitgevers in de Zestiende Eeuw* (Amsterdam, 1900–1915).

MPM: Antwerp, Museum Plantin-Moretus.

Oxford, U.P.: Oxford, University Press.

PRO: London, Public Record Office.

RDB: C. Ruelens and A. de Backer, *Annales Plantiniennes* (Brussels, 1865).

Rothschild: *Catalogue des livres composant la bibliothèque de feu M. le baron James de Rothschild* (Paris, 1884–1920).

Rotterdam: Rotterdam, Gemeentelijke Bibliotheek.

Sabbe: M. Sabbe, 'Bijdrage tot de Bibliographie van Ameet Tavernier', *De Gulden Passer*, 7 (Antwerp, 1929), pp. 168–201; 8 (1930), pp. 181–2.

Sabbe–Audin: M. Sabbe and M. Audin, *Die Civilité-Schriften des Robert Granjon und die flämischen Drucker des 16. Jahrhunderts* (Vienna, 1929).

STC: A. W. Pollard, G. R. Redgrave, and others, *Short-Title Catalogue of Books printed in England, Scotland, & Ireland and of English Books printed abroad 1475–1640* (1926).

The Hague: The Hague, Koninklijke Bibliotheek.

Vanderhaeghen: F. Vanderhaeghen, *Bibliographie gantoise* (Ghent, 1856–69).

Van Heurck: E. H. van Heurck, *Voyage autour de ma bibliothèque: livres populaires et livres d'école flamands* (Antwerp, 1927).

Vervliet: H. D. L. Vervliet, 'Rectifications et additions à la bibliographie d'Aimé Tavernier, imprimeur et tailleur de caractères anversois', *Gutenberg Jahrbuch*, 36 (Mainz, 1961), pp. 121–8.

Waller: E. Dronckers, *Verzameling F. G. Waller: Catalogus van Nederlandsche en Vlaamsche Populaire Boeken* (The Hague, 1936).

Wing: D. Wing, *Short-Title Catalogue of Books printed in England . . . 1641–1700* (New York, 1945–51).

Zurich: Zurich, Zentralbibliothek.

I

PRELIMINARY

ETTERS form so large a part of everyday experience that after a brief apprenticeship in early life modern man develops a time-saving mechanism for extracting meaning from them with the least attention to their forms.[1] Anyone, however, can see a difference between Civilité types and other types for the Latin alphabet—a difference striking enough to make books printed in them stand out as a well-defined class. It is a class of curiosa to which book-collectors have long been attracted, and the catalogues of antiquarian booksellers by often reproducing pages set in Civilité have made the types and their name familiar to readers who do not as a rule concern themselves with the distinctions of typography. Whether one likes the types or not is a matter of being able to look at them with any eye but that of a reader. It is no wonder if they are graceful, for they are renderings by the most skilful letter-cutters in the golden age of the art of a handwriting perfected by calligraphers when writing was a highly refined and much esteemed accomplishment. Illegible they certainly are to modern eyes, but the uses to which they were put within the past hundred years prove clearly enough that our difficulty in reading them is due to a specialized training.

The State of Knowledge

It is not surprising that the literature about these types began with studies addressed to book-collectors. As long ago as 1850, when founts of Civilité in a sadly dilapidated state still did duty in provincial printing-offices, Baron Jérôme Pichon wrote an article on their use in sixteenth-century books.[2] Thirty years later Alcide Bonneau compiled a

[1] The initial is copied from a book (No. 465 in the Appendix) printed at Caen, probably about 1775, where it is in a poor condition indicative of a great age.

[2] 'Du Caractère dit de civilité et les livres qui ont été imprimés avec ce caractère au XVIe siècle', *Mélanges de littérature et d'histoire recueillis et publiés par la Société des Bibliophiles françois* (Paris, 1850), pp. 330–7. He stops at 1562.

list of works set in them reaching up to his own day.[1] More recently a Belgian author has discussed their part in the make-up of popular books and school books in his country.[2] Interest in the history and design of the types themselves is more modern. Scientific treatment of the subject began in 1907 with an article by Leonard Willems,[3] and in 1921 Maurits Sabbe and Marius Audin published their book on *Caractères de Civilité* with numerous illustrations and specimens.[4] Their book in a German translation with revisions by the authors, published, in an edition limited to 270 copies, at Vienna in 1929, has since been the standard work on the types and their uses.[5] Alice Hulubei has supplemented it where books in French are concerned,[6] and two studies by Professor H. de la Fontaine Verwey of Civilité types and their part in Protestant propaganda are recent and valuable additions.[7]

The information to be found in these books and in more general histories of typography[8] might well be thought enough; but in our attempts to identify and catalogue the relics of Civilité types at the Museum Plantin-Moretus at Antwerp and in the collection of Messrs. Enschedé at Haarlem we have found that it does not account for nearly all the facts. There are many more types of the kind than was supposed, and some that were regarded as distinct are found to be mutilated duplicates of others or to have interesting relationships with them.

To gain an idea of the scope and importance of the subject we have made a list of books printed in Civilité types.[9] It is far from being complete, but it will provide some statistical grounds for

[1] *La Civilité puérile par Erasme de Rotterdam, précédée d'une notice sur les livres de civilité* (Paris, 1877). See also M. Heine, 'Les Caractères de civilité', *Bulletin du bibliophile et du bibliothécaire*, N.S. viii (Paris, 1921), pp. 468–71.

[2] E. van Heurck, *Voyage autour de ma bibliothèque: livres populaires et livres de l'école flamands* (Antwerp, 1924).

[3] 'Ameet Tavernier en de Invoering van de Civilité-letter in Zuid-Nederland', *Tijdschrift voor Boek- en Bibliotheekwezen*, 5 (The Hague, 1907), pp. 241–63.

[4] *Les Caractères de civilité de Robert Granjon et les imprimeurs flamands* (Lyons, 1921).

[5] *Die Civilité-Schriften des Robert Granjon in Lyon und die flämischen Drucker des 16. Jahrhunderts* (Vienna, 1929).

[6] 'Les Caractères de civilité', *Arts et métiers graphiques*, 21 (Paris, 1930–1), pp. 127–34.

[7] 'Typografische Schrijfboeken: een Hoofdstuk uit de Geschiedenis van de Civilité-letter', *De Gulden Passer*, 39 (Antwerp, 1962), pp. 288–362. 'Les Caractères de civilité et la propagande religieuse', *Bibliothèque d'humanisme et renaissance, Travaux et documents*, t. xxvi (Geneva, 1964), pp. 7–27.

[8] Especially A. F. Johnson, *Type Designs, their History and Development*, 2nd ed. (London, 1959), pp. 132–46; Stanley Morison, 'On Script Types', *The Fleuron*, iv (London, 1925), pp. 1–42, slightly amplified as *Caractères de l'écriture dans la typographie* (Paris, 1927). There are useful notes in *Catalogue of Typefounders' Specimens*, &c. Birrell & Garnett Ltd. (London, 1928).   [9] The Appendix to this volume.

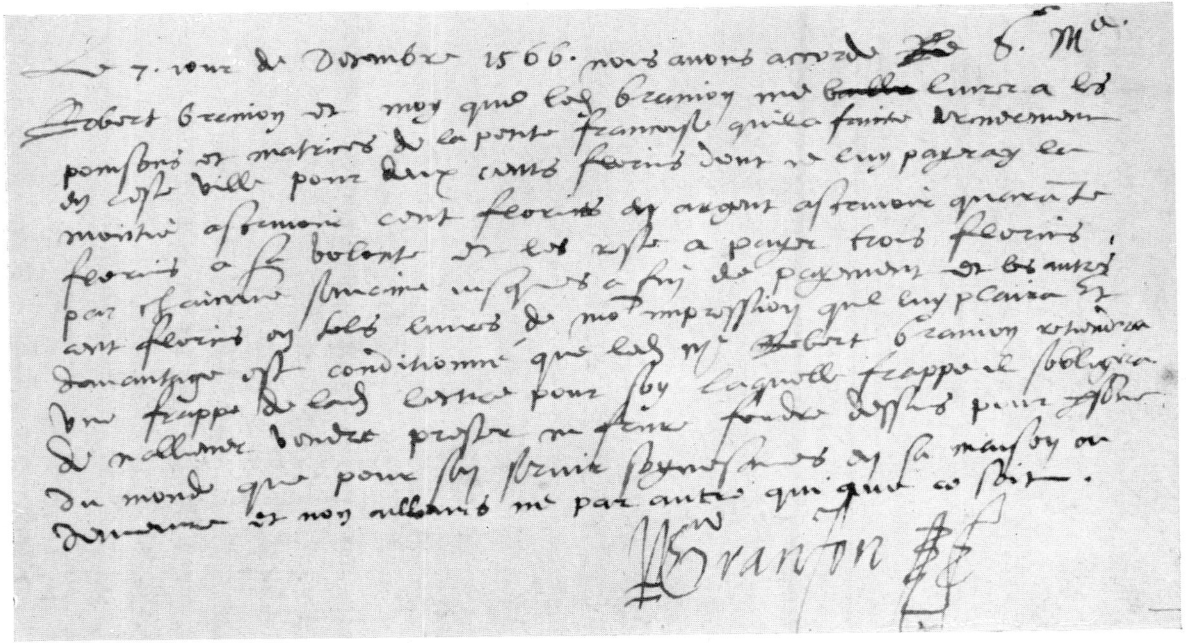

FIG. 1. The French *lettre courante*. The entry in Plantin's accounts of an agreement between him and Robert Granjon for the purchase of punches and matrices for a 'lettre françoise' on the body of *Garamonde* or *Petit romain*. 1566

Fig. 2. A Flemish hand. A writ from the chancery of the Netherlands, dated at Arras 1541 (part)

Fig. 3. The English Secretary hand. A teller's slip from the Royal Exchequer (part), 1568

an estimate of the part they played in the history of society and of printing.

We ourselves are attracted to this subject mainly by a desire to learn about the letter-designers, letter-cutters, and typefounders of the sixteenth and seventeenth centuries. Some of the best work of gifted artists such as Robert Granjon, Hendrik van den Keere, Philippe Danfrie, and Ameet Tavernier was done in perfecting this kind of letter, and without a knowledge of it no estimate of the typographical trades of that time can be just.

The Handwriting

We are concerned essentially with types rendering a cursive hand of the sixteenth century in a calligraphic form. Special characteristics of this hand, sloped, rather long, descenders and an r whose first stroke leans backwards, appear in French documents of the late fourteenth century;[1] and before the middle of the fifteenth century a recognizable style of writing in which the letter forms were adapted to make the pen's passage from one to the next easier than it had been in earlier Latin scripts had been developed in France and was in use for correspondence and notes[2] and for the less elaborate kinds of books.[3] Polished examples of it can be found about that time.[4] The spread of this hand to the Burgundian Low Countries[5] and to England[6] may be dated roughly in the last quarter of the fifteenth century. By the time it was brought into typography (1557) it was evidently a highly artificial accomplishment.[7]

[1] An example written in 1375 is in Ch. Samaran and R. Marichal, *Catalogue des manuscrits en écriture latine portant des indications de date, de lieu, ou de copiste* (Paris, 1959–62), vol. i, pl. lv.

[2] For example pp. 54, 55 (1436) of *Umbrae codicum occidentalium*, iii. *Registrum autographum priorum Collegii Sorbonae* (Amsterdam, 1960).

[3] e.g. Samaran and Marichal, op. cit., vol. i, pl. cxiii (1456).

[4] Examples in M. Prou, *Manuel de paléographie, Recueil de facsimilés d'écriture du Ve au XVIIe siècle* (Paris, 1904), pl. 36 (Château-Thierry, 1436), 37 (Paris, 1446).

[5] See the essay by G. I. Lieftinck in *Colloques internationaux du Centre National de la Recherche Scientifique: Sciences humaines*, iv. *Nomenclature des écritures livresques du IXe au XVIe siècle* (Paris, 1954). Some examples are in H. Delitsch, *Geschichte der abendländischen Schreibschriftformen* (Leipzig, 1928), Abb. 59d (Flemish, 1468), 59e (Burgundian, 1479).

[6] Hilary Jenkinson, 'Elizabethan Handwritings, a Preliminary Sketch', *The Library*, 4th ser., iii (London, 1923), pp. 1–34; the same writer's 'English Current Writing and Early Printing', *Transactions of the Bibliographical Society*, iii (London, 1916), pp. 273–95. An example of 1468 is in Delitsch, 58c.

[7] In 1922 an expert wrote: 'Personne, que nous sachions, n'a cherché à analyser et à définir avec précision les caractères de ces écritures' (Ch. Samaran, 'Note pour servir au déchiffrement de la cursive gothique de la fin du xve à la fin du xviie siècle', *Le Moyen Âge*, xxxiv (Paris, 1922), at p. 97. Many more reproductions have since become available but there is still little guidance for the layman.

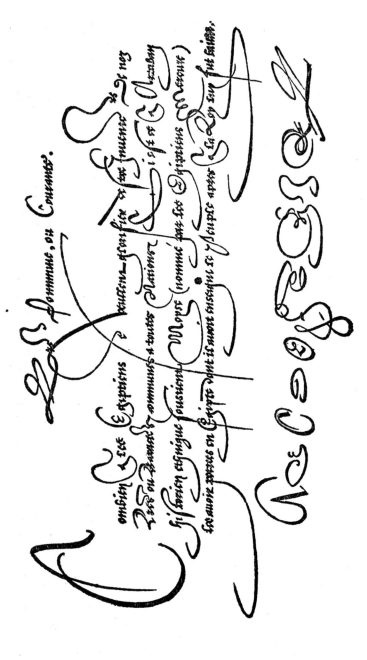

Fig. 4. A model for the 'lettre commune ou courante' in Pierre Hamon's *Alphabet de linuention de lettres en diuerses escritures*, Paris, 1561.

This *lettre courante* varied with the writer's circumstances, his cultural inheritance, and his profession. In ceremonious use it was upright, but when written informally it was sloped and some letters were linked. French scribes knew, or invented, a good many slightly different forms of it. Models for them in Pierre Hamon's writing manual of 1561[1] are headed: Carree, Ancienne, Commune ou Courante, d'Estat, Ronde, de Comptes, Mignardee, and Secretarienne ou Financiere. The edition of 1566[2] adds more, including a Palaceale.

When Robert Granjon made his first type for this current hand he called it 'lettre françoise', and by that name his and similar typefaces were known to later French typefounders. The earlier use of the expression is unknown to us; it appears to have been a generic name used to distinguish scripts of medieval French ancestry from the humanistic,[3] and perhaps it was Granjon who first attached it to the *courante* in particular. In his *Champ Fleury* (1529) Geoffroi Tory regards four styles of writing as being 'lettres françoises': the *lettre de forme*, the *lettre bastarde*, the *lettre tourneure*, and *lettres de cadeaulx*—the whole Gothic repertory, excepting the cursive, which, we may suppose, Tory disregarded as being too informal for his purposes, which, broadly speaking, were architectural. Forty years later the scribe impersonated in Plantin's *Dialogues francois pour les ieunes enfans*[4] distinguishes the informal hand as 'la commune courante'.

It appears to have been John Baildon who first published the name 'Secretary' for the corresponding English style of writing[5] and so provided a label for the types rendering it.[6] The Dutch and Flemings

[1] *L'Alphabet de linuention de lettres en diuerses escritures* (Paris, J. Le Royer, 1561), BM, 1268. a. 5.

[2] BN, Rés. pV, 404. In Germany Wolffgang Fugger showed various styles of Currentschrift—gelegt, geschoben, gewunden, and gewelbt—in *Ein nutzlich und wohlgegrundt Formular manncherley schöner Schrieften* (Nuremberg, 1553).

[3] Tagliente in *Opera che insegna a scrivere*, first published at Venice in 1524, gives the name *francescha* (in later editions *francese*) to a model for *textura*; Palatino (Rome, 1545) and Cresci (Rome, 1570) use the name *lettere francesi* for the Gothic cursive; and Yciar (Saragossa, 1559) shows a *bastarda* by the name of *Letra francesa redonda y triada*. Later French writing-masters, Étienne de Blégny, 1712, and Étienne Royllet, 1735, divide the hands into *françoise* and *italienne*.

[4] *La Premiere et la seconde partie des dialogues francois pour les ieunes enfans* (Antwerp, Plantin, 1567), at p. 232.

[5] Jean de Beauchesne and John Baildon, *A Booke containing divers Sortes of Hands* (London, 1570 or 1571): 'as well the English as French Secretarie with the Italian, Roman, Chancelry and Court hands'.

[6] Applied by Thomas Hearne to Granjon's first script type: *Remarks and Collections of Thomas Hearne*, iii, Oxford Historical Society (Oxford, 1889), p. 86 (1710), and by John James to the similar face in his foundry: *A Catalogue and Specimen of the Printing-Type-Foundry of Mr. John James* (London, 1782).

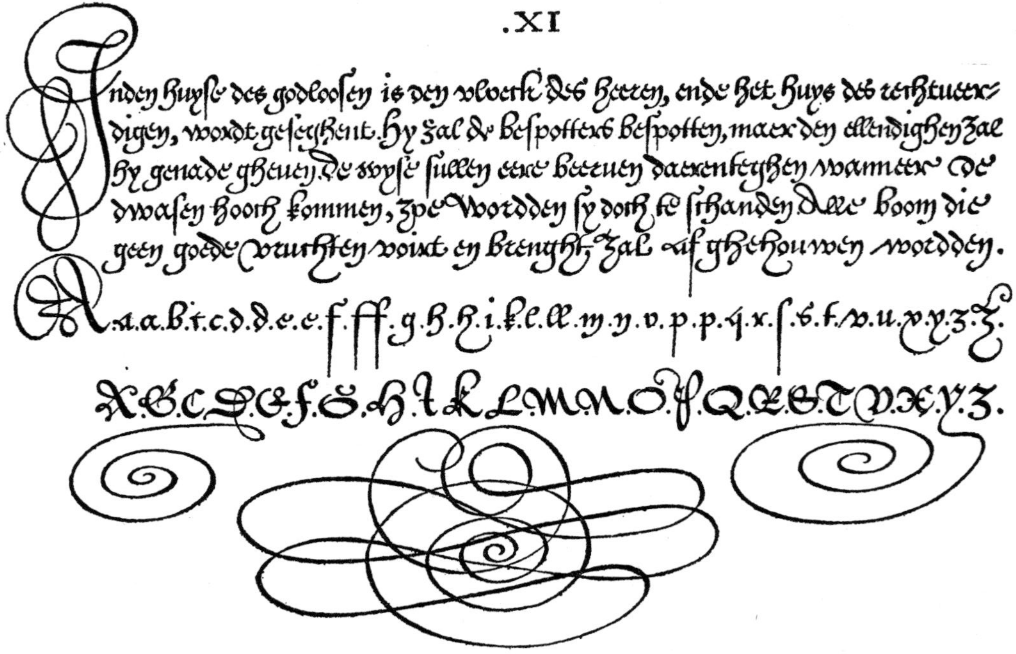

FIG. 5. A model for the Flemish cursive hand in Clement Perret's *Exercitatio alphabetica nova et utilissima*, Antwerp, 1569.

had no such specific name but called their types of the kind 'script' (*geschreven letter*). National peculiarities in the written hand led expert scribes to provide special models for a 'litera Belgica' and a 'litera Anglica'.[1]

The French *lettre courante* had much affinity with its Gothic relation, the *bâtarde*. 'Bâtarde' (*bastarda*, Bastard Secretary) meant different things to succeeding generations of writers, but always until the seventeenth century a Gothic script intermediate in formality between *textura* and the cursive. The *bâtarde* and the *courante* had the capital letters in common, and some of the minuscules (b d f g h i l) were the same in both. Since the invention of printing the *bâtarde* had met the need for a book-script popular and familiar enough for matter in the modern languages, or in Latin if it were addressed to the lower orders of society. A type of the kind was the first or the second to be seen in print (in the Mainz 30-line Letter of Indulgence, 1454–5), and as the hand was reformed and refined new types were cut for it. A type for the *bâtarde* in its mid-fifteenth-century form was sponsored by Caxton about 1474,[2] and types of a similar kind were commonly used in France, the southern Netherlands, and England for the next fifty years. An unusually calligraphic type of this class used by Guillaume Le Talleur of Rouen about 1490 is familiar to English students of printing because of its occurrence in Littleton's *Tenores* and Statham's *Abridgement*.[3]

By 1550 the *bâtarde* printing types were too old-fashioned. It is hard to find books printed in them in France after that date—a few, mostly from Rouen—and their use in England ended about then. In the Dutch-speaking Netherlands it was a style rarely seen: a Bible was printed by Cornelis Henriczoon at Delft in 1524 in a face intermediate between a French *bâtarde* and a Schwabacher.[4] In writing the *bâtarde* survived to give stateliness and emphasis, in accordance with an old practice of calligraphers,[5] to the headings and opening phrases of

---

[1] [Simone Verovio?] *Essemplari di xiiii lingue principalissime* [Rome?, 1592] has an example of 'Belgica' with 'Alphabeto di Fiamenghi' and 'Anglica' with 'Alphabetum Anglicum'. Judocus Hondius, *Theatrum artis scribendi* (Leyden, 1594), shows hands of the *courante* kind as 'Alphabetum flandricum', 'Litera anglicana', and 'Françoyse'.

[2] *British Museum Catalogue of Books printed in the XVth Century*, Part IX (London, 1962), p. 129, pl. 1 B.

[3] Ibid., Part VIII (1949), pl. lxvi.

[4] W. Nijhoff, *Art typographique dans les Pays-Bas pendant les années 1500–1540* (The Hague, vol. i, 1926), s.v. 'Delft, Cornelis Henriczoon Lettersnijder', pl. II, III, nos. 9, 11.

[5] E. Maunde Thompson, in *Bibliographica*, 3 (London, 1897), at p. 272, writing of the ninth century: 'The penmen of Tours produced two styles of hands: one of a more ornamental character, and employed by them in important or prominent parts of the text, . . . the other less elaborate . . . .'

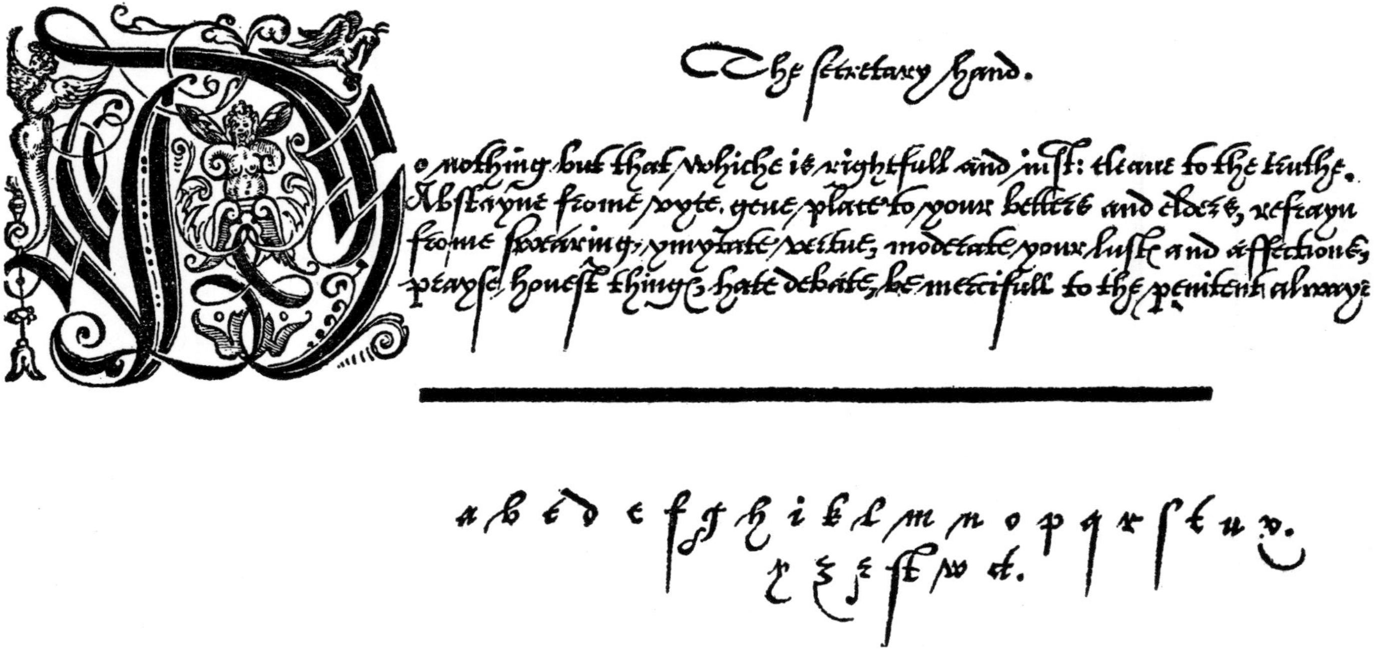

The Secretarie hande.

Fig. 6. A model for the Secretary hand in Jean de Beauchesne and John Baildon's *Booke containing divers sortes of hands*, London, 1571.

documents penned in the *courante*, a practice which printers who adopted Civilité types felt bound to imitate. In this restricted use *bâtarde* types survived their disappearance from the texts of books, and some were cut specially for it in the second half of the sixteenth century.

In general, however, script types in the medieval tradition must have seemed to belong to the past in 1557; and until Granjon cut a type for it in that year nobody expected to see the French cursive in a printed book.[1]

The hand represented by Granjon's type ceased to be written in France about the middle of the seventeenth century,[2] when it gave way to its descendant, the *financière*, and to a rounded Italic, the *Italienne bâtarde*; nevertheless our Appendix shows that French children were expected to read it, at least, until late in the nineteenth century. In the Low Countries the related hand survived as 'lettering', a carefully formed hand for notices and ornamental writing. There also it was taught to children well into the nineteenth century.[3] In England schoolmasters insisted on Secretary for the mother tongue in the early part of the seventeenth century,[4] and models for it were provided in the editions of Edmund Coote's *English School-master* as late as that of 1673; but in the 42nd, of 1684, an Italian hand was substituted. Not long after that the informal 'running' Secretary drops out of the expert penman's manuals,[5] and the hand, in its 'set' form, survived only in legal and official documents, from which it was finally banished some sixty years ago.[6]

The Name 'Civilité'

This name for the types is by now unavoidable. French printers were using it by the eighteenth century: thus Claude Lamesle of

---

[1] Granjon had previously cut a few letters of the *courante* minuscule alphabet to serve for tablatures of the lute and the cithern. These can be seen in Simon Gorlier, *Troisieme livre contenant plusieurs duos et trios* (Paris, R. Granjon and M. Fezandat, 1551), and Albert de Rippe de Mantoue, *Premier livre de tablature de leut* (Paris, M. Fezandat, 1553).

[2] The change has been ascribed largely to the influence of the writing manual, *Les Œuvres*, by Lucas Materot, published at Avignon in 1608: Stanley Morison, *Latin Script since the Renaissance* (Cambridge, 1938), p. 10. See the same writer 'On Script Types', *The Fleuron*, iv. 10–15. M. Prou, *Manuel de paléographie* (Paris, 1924), says that conservative Frenchmen, lawyers especially, wrote the Gothic *courante* until the end of the century.   [3] Cf. *Het Boek*, 18 (1929), p. 361.

[4] John Brindley, *Ludus literarius, or the Grammar Schoole* (1612), p. 31. The use of Secretary in school is evidently assumed in *G.D.'s Directions for Writing 1656* (privately reprinted with an introduction by Stanley Morison, Cambridge, 1933).

[5] A late example is in T. Ollyffe's *Practical Penman* (1713); but the dating of these books and the plates in them is difficult.

[6] L. C. Hector, *The Handwriting of English Documents* (London, 1958), pp. 57–58, 64.

Paris in his typefounder's specimen book of 1742 and his successors, the firm of Gando, after him, and the Belgian typefounder J. F. Rosart in his specimens issued at Brussels in 1768. By that time the older name 'lettre françoise' had attached itself to later scripts. The general acceptance of the name 'Civilité' for the types is probably attributable to Brunet's *Manuel du libraire*, first published in 1810, where the courtesy books for children so often set in these types are listed under the article 'Civilité'. *De civilitate morum puerorum libellus* by Erasmus[1] was the pioneer work on this theme, and the little books in modern languages adapted from his by various authors had titles reminiscent of their original. In France, where these books were more beloved than elsewhere and went on being used much longer, the best-known was *La Civilité puérile*, a title given at various times to various adaptations of the book by Erasmus.[2]

The first of such books to be set in Civilité type (our frontispiece reproduces the title-page) was printed by Granjon at Lyons in 1558 (4),[3] and it was followed by another printed in Paris by Philippe Danfrie and Richard Breton in 1559 (28) and a Flemish one published at Antwerp (17) in the same year.[4] Later in the century Mahiel du Bois printed the *Civilité* in Paris for Claude Micard (212). Thereafter there were frequent editions both in Paris and in the provinces, and it is safe to assume that any list of them that can be made now must be unfairly weighted in favour of the later ones.

[1] Antwerp, M. Hillen, 1530. In later editions the title was altered to *Civilitas morum*. See J. Le Coultre, *Maturin Cordier et les origines de la pédagogie française, 1530–1564* (Neuchâtel, 1926), pp. 344–7.

[2] Bibliographical studies have been published lately of one of these by Jean-Baptiste de la Salle, first printed in 1703 and constantly reprinted in France during the 18th and 19th centuries: F. Albert-Valentin (of the Frères des Écoles chrétiennes), *Édition critique des Règles de la Bienséance et de la Civilité chrétienne* (Paris, 1955), pp. 513–19; L'Institut des Frères des Écoles chrétiennes, *Les Règles de la Bienséance et de la Civilité chrétienne* (Cahiers Lasalliens, Rome, 1965), pp. iii–xii. These authorities cite editions unknown to us and not included in our Appendix.

[3] The numbers in brackets refer to the list of books in the Appendix.

[4] We have been unable to verify the existence of an edition at Antwerp by Jean Bellere, 1559, cited by Brunet and later writers as the first in Civilité type.

II

HISTORY OF PRINTING IN
CIVILITÉ TYPES

The First Civilité Type

IT was in France that the first type for this handwriting was made. That might as well be explained by the relatively advanced state of typography in France as by any special demand there for a type of the kind. In 1557, at Lyons, Robert Granjon published a small book, *Dialogue de la vie et de la mort* by Innocenzio Ringhieri, translated by Jean Louveau (see fig. 7), and in his dedicatory address to the Chevalier d'Urfé prefacing the text Granjon explains the use of a new script type which he had cut.

When I call to mind [Granjon wrote] how Hebrews, Greeks, Romans, and even some barbarous nations took such care of their own languages that they scrupled and thought it a shame to use letters found out by any people but their own, I could but blush for the heedlessness in this respect of our forebears; for they, possessing the wherewithal to dispense with help from others, yet preferred to borrow from neighbours. It is a thing to be deplored all the more for our French character (which we have been fortunate beyond our deserts to preserve) proving, when compared with others, to be in no way inferior to them. . . .

Having before now cut various fair characters (some not yet brought to the light of day, others still a-forging), I set myself to cut our French alphabet, justify the matrices, cast it, and lastly dress the type ready for printing, so that I have been able with it to print this Dialogue, hoping, if it be the will of God and our lord the King, to complete another type for the same, on a bigger body and far more handsome. . . .[1]

[1] 'Car en me proposant deuant les yeux combien les Hebrieux, les Grecs, les Latins, voyre plusieurs peuples barbares, ont esté curieux de leur propre langue iusques à faire conscience, et tenir à honte de se seruir des lettres par autres que par eux inventees, Je ne pouuois non rougir, de la negligence de nos Maieurs en cest endroit, qui ayans de quoy se passer de leurs voisins, ont mieux ayme estre leurs redevables, que de s'ayder de leur propre: chose d'autant plus à deplourer, que si lon confere nos caracteres Francoys (qui ne scay comment nous sont demeurez saufs) à ceux de toutes autres nations, on trouuera qu'ilz ne leur cedent en rien . . . apres auoir taillé plusieurs beaux caracteres, dont les vns n'ont encore este en lumiere, les autres sont encores sur la forge, Je me suis mis à tailler nostre lettre Francoyse, iustifier les Matrices, en faire la fonte, et finablement la rendre propre à l'Imprimerie: sy que i'en ay imprimé ce present dialogue de la Vie & de la Mort, esperant s'il plaist a Dieu et au Roy nostre Sire, d'en acheuer vne autre de

Fig. 7. *Dialogue de la vie et de la mort*, Lyons, R. Granjon, 1557. Title-page and first page of the dedication. Type A1.

Robert Granjon was born in Paris about 1513,[1] the son of a printer and bookseller. He must have begun cutting punches for type at an early age, for an Italic attributable to him was in use in 1543.[2] He had his own shop in Paris by 1545,[3] and in 1549 he began publishing, at first by himself and later in partnership with Michel Fezandat, with whom he was associated until 1551. Before 1547 he, being then in Paris, had supplied matrices or type to Jean de Tournes and to Sebastien Gryphius at Lyons. His establishment in that city, where he married the daughter of Bernard Salomon the artist, cannot have been long before the publication there of three books with his imprint in 1557. All his life he was migratory between Paris, Lyons, Antwerp, and Frankfurt; as late as 1575 he owned a house in Paris, and he is believed to have ended his days in Rome.[4] He had a wonderfully large output of punches and matrices for Roman, Italic, Greek, Syriac, and Arabic types, besides his scripts, much of it prior to the year 1557.

We may regard Granjon, then, as primarily a highly-skilled artisan and read his reasons for cutting the *lettre françoise* as those of a man concerned more with type than with the history of handwriting. The new type-face was an attractive novelty, beautifully cut and founded. Granjon was one of the two or three greatest masters of letter-cutting, and his *lettre françoise* is informed by his superb style as well as by his technical proficiency. Artistically the fount is a brilliant success.

The type has severe handicaps, and Granjon must have known it,

plus gros corps, et beaucoup plus belle.' *Dialogue de la vie et de la La Mort, Composé en Toscan par Maistre Innocent Ringhiere Gentilhomme Boulongnois. Nouuellement traduit en Francoys par Jehan Louueau Recteur de Chastillon de dombes.* A Lyon. De l'Imprimerie de Robert GranJon. Mil. Vᶜ. Lvij. Sign. a2ᵛ–a3ʳ. The Bibliothèque Nationale has a copy dated in that year (1): a copy at the Bodleian Library is dated in 1558 (10).

Allegations that Granjon's first Civilité type had been used before publication of the *Dialogue* (1557) have not been substantiated. The 'Civilité puérile' of 1556 attributed to Granjon by Karl Faulmann (*Illustrierte Geschichte der Buchdruckerkunst*, Vienna, 1882, p. 286) cannot be traced. The placing of an illustration on p. 375 of Alfred Cartier, *Bibliographie des éditions des De Tournes* (Lyon, 1937–8) might mislead a reader into thinking that type of this kind had been used in 1554 (No. 284), whereas the reproduction is of a later edition (No. 757, p. 688, of the year 1609).

[1] A specimen of his Arabic cut by command of Pope Gregory XIII has under it the printed legend: 'Rob. GranIon Parisien. Typographus & Characterum incisor. incidebat Romae. 1583. aetatis suae. lxx.' For this information we are indebted to Mr. James Mosley of the St. Bride Institute, London. Granjon's parentage is reported by S.-P. Fournier le Jeune, *Manuel typographique*, vol. ii, Paris 1766.

[2] A. F. Johnson, *Type Designs, their History and Development*, 2nd ed. London, 1959, p. 112.

[3] Ibid., p. 111.

[4] Baudrier, vol. ii, pp. 49–64, vol. i, pp. 284–5; P. Renouard, 'Imprimeurs parisiens, libraires, fondeurs ...', *Revue des bibliothèques*, 34 (Paris, 1924), pp. 178–9.

enough to make printers loath to invest in it and to account to some extent for the limited use to which this and other designs like it were put. The first Civilité had at least 138 sorts, as compared with some 120 usual at the time for Roman or Italic, and the Civilité had no small capitals and, as a rule, no numerals. An average total for a Black Letter reproducing the *textura* book hand was 90. The thirty ligatures of the *françoise* compare with about twenty normally supplied for the Roman, and in addition it required two dozen extra sorts for the initial, final, and other alternative forms of the lower-case letters. These last were a tax on the time of the punchcutter, typefounder, and compositor. Like all Gothic scripts made into type, this one suffered from having fine minims projecting from the letters on either side, making the type difficult to cast and to rub and quick to show wear. More than all this, it was poor value in legibility for the space it occupied.

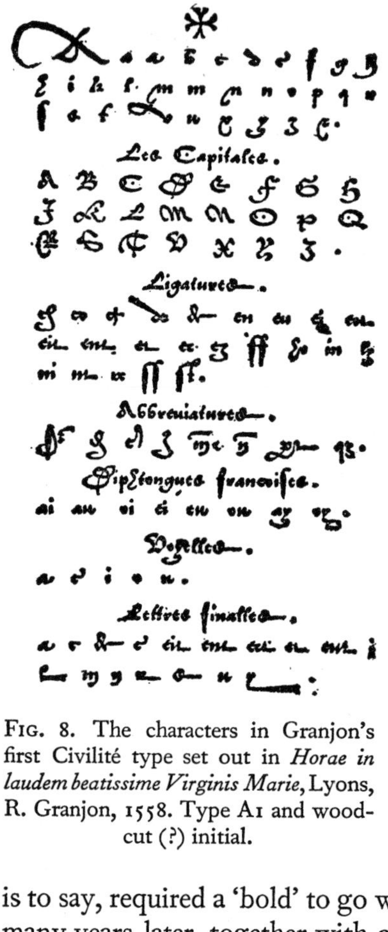

Moreover, as an equipment for printing in a manner imitating current Gothic handwriting this one type was inadequate. The habit of scribes and scriveners of writing headings and exordia in another, bolder, style of letter has been mentioned above. The text letter, that

FIG. 8. The characters in Granjon's first Civilité type set out in *Horae in laudem beatissime Virginis Marie*, Lyons, R. Granjon, 1558. Type A1 and woodcut (?) initial.

is to say, required a 'bold' to go with it. This Granjon provided a good many years later, together with a 'semi-bold', a face intermediate between the other two in weight and formality. The books in Civilité type by Philippe Danfrie and Richard Breton have large and bold letters of two sizes in the *bâtarde* convention, capitals and minuscules, for the headings and introductory words. They are rather roughly cut and unevenly spaced and are probably castings in sand moulds from woodcut originals (Fig. 31). Big cursive initial letters, some of them apparently cut in wood, occur in many of the books set in Civilité types. It was a style involving quite a large outlay of capital.

The Justification for a Gothic Script Type

Granjon must have been aware of currents in the thoughts of his countrymen favouring a national form of printing type, for that was the only argument he used to recommend his new fount. The slight success of the *lettre françoise* as a text type, slighter in France than in the Low Countries, shows that currents of the kind were not strong or were met by some that were stronger. In the year of the liberation of Calais it must be supposed that an appeal to patriotism would be powerful. In the resolve to make the vernacular a competitor with Latin for serious books and in the programmes of the time for a literature in French and for reforming and regularizing the language, guarding it from excess of latinity or italicism, there was some purely nationalist sentiment. One of the manifestoes, the *Devis de la langue francoise* by Abel Matthieu (25, 42), was originally set in Civilité type. And even in the *Deffence et illustration de la langue francoise*, issuing from the Pléiade and so far removed from popular nationalism, there is a sentence that could be read as favouring a national form for letters.[1]

Without dispute, the *lettre françoise* was a national handwriting. Robert Estienne affirmed it in the year of Granjon's essay in bringing it into print. In his *Traicte de la grammaire françoise* he wrote: 'We have our peculiar forms for the letters, not far removed from those of the Italians; but they do not slope forward as theirs do, but are upright like the Roman and fatter. The bodies of our letters are short, and the heads and tails long.'[2] In the original edition, of 1557, he illustrates the passage with an alphabet in *bâtarde*, but his son, reprinting it in 1569 (121), substituted Civilité, which accords better with the sense of the text. French humanists, though they wrote Latin in Italic, wrote their mother tongue in the *courante*.[3] When the Civilité types were no longer a novelty, they were sometimes used by reputable printers to

---

[1] '... afin que presens, absens, vyfs, & mors manifestans l'vn a l'autre le secret de notz coeurs, plus facilement paruenions a notre propre felicite, qui gist en l'intelligence des Sciences, non point au son des Paroles: et par consequent celles langues, & celles Ecritures deuroient plus estre en vsaige, lesquelles on apprendroit plus facilement': edition of 1549, Part i, p. 10.

[2] 'Nous avons forme de lettres particulieres, approchantes assez pres de celles des Italiens, mais elles ne sont point ainsi couchees sur le devant, ains sont droictes comme les Romaines, & plus grasses: le corps de lettres est court, les iambes et les testes longues': edition of 1557, p. 5.

[3] M. Prou, *Manuel de paléographie* (Paris, 1924), p. 253. Ch. Beaulieux, *Histoire de l'orthographie française* (Paris, 1927), p. 254. It was usual in western Europe as a whole: G. Mentz, *Handschriften der Reformationszeit* (Bonn, 1912).

stress the Frenchness of parallel versions or of quoted matter: examples, however, are rare.[1]

It is not surprising that a type imitating handwriting was welcomed for certain purposes for reasons quite other than those advanced by Granjon in its favour. To be addressed in manuscript is a compliment, and pseudo-manuscript had about it an allusion to the handwritten books presented to the most eminent patrons.[2] Printers, for their part, have a need for a distinguishing type: it serves to mark the separateness of forewords and dedications and to add grace and variety to headings and titles. Such judicious printers as Jean de Tournes, Christophe Plantin, and Willem Silvius turned the Civilité to good account for ornamenting their books. It seems not to have suffered from the re-proach of being 'Gothic', a word that by 1540 was being used comically and contemptuously.[3] Rabelais wrote French in Secretary, and it is hard to believe that he would have told us that Gargantua was taught 'à escripre Gotticquement' if he had thought he did so himself. In any case, the average Frenchman wanted the prettiest things from both worlds, in architecture the gargoyles and crockets as well as the five orders, in literature Amadis and Palmerin as well as Plutarch.

To a large number of readers the type seemed legible. There is contemporary testimony to this in the foreword to the *Alexandreïs* printed by Granjon in 1558 (6), following closely upon the *Dialogue de la vie et de la mort*. Introducing the book, R. Constantinus[4] praises the type in Latin to this effect:

The novelty and strangeness of these letters will certainly surprise the reader, but I dare say he will be as much delighted by their clearness and elegance. Not only did Robert Granjon print them, but, like another Dibutades, the potter of Sicyon, he made a mould and produced castings in it. In point of beauty and legibility these letters are not outdone by others, and they are familiar to us because they imitate the written hand. What is printed looks like writing, and it may be hard to tell that the page is printed with type. Foreigners may like them as well as we, for reasons which I leave to the writing-masters, though without such recommendation experience of the letters will of itself prove their merit. Soon they will lose their novelty and become generally familiar; for in these days, for the most part, people

---

[1] The French examples in Théodore de Bèze, *De Francicae linguae recta pronunciatione* (Geneva, E. Vignon, 1584); the French version in *Le Galathée* (Geneva, J. de Tournes II, 1598). Other examples are in 265, 304, printed by De Tournes II.

[2] Alice Hulubei, op. cit., p. 127. She calls Civilité 'un alphabet de déférence'.

[3] Rabelais, ii, ch. x; i, ch. xiv.

[4] Probably Robert, the son of Antoine Constantin, printer of Lyons. He was a school-master at Montauban. See *Dictionnaire de biographie française*, ix (Paris, 1961), pp. 517–18.

in Europe can write. Let no one despise the things of his country and admire what is foreign, for the ancient Romans rightly thought it a crime punishable by banishment . . . and he is a bad citizen who loves another country better than his own.

To the slow or occasional reader and to the beginner no doubt it was an advantage to be confronted by the letters that he wrote, and for such the Civilité types were reserved increasingly as time went on. Not only school books, courtesy and morality books, but official forms and notices were set in these types in order to reach the widest public; and more would have been printed in them if more printers had stocked them. The earlier history of typography makes it clear that every kind of reader had to be wooed in the script most familiar to him, and as publishing increased in volume specialization proceeded. The last 'victories of calligraphy over print'[1] had been in 1498 and 1500 when Aldus perfected his cursive Greek and introduced his Italic. In 1557 children were given a type of their own. However, association with them spoiled a chance of success with readers of other kinds.

It does not surprise a generation accustomed to find printers' letters easy to read and handwriting difficult that Civilité failed as a type for texts. As Gothic types acquired a 'popular' character,[2] about 1530, printers in France followed the Italian example and began setting their own language in Roman. The change is not well documented.[3] Probably a critical point was passed when Denys Janot, 'Imprimeur du roi pour la langue françoise', issued the first Book of *Amadis* in Roman type in 1540. Geoffroi Tory, though he did not (as is sometimes said) advocate the use of Roman type in his *Champ Fleury*, did so by his example in publishing French texts in it from 1529 onwards.[4]

More than all the influence of the humanists and the precepts of experts in the decorative arts familiarity with printed books must have led to acceptance of the Roman alphabet for the northern languages. There is a sense in which a β c can be called more rational than a b c; but there is no doubt that A B C are better than λ ℬ φ. So far as capitals are concerned, printing freed the essential forms from incumbrances accumulated during an age of writing. It had more difficulty

---

[1] A. Dain, *Les Manuscrits* (Paris 1949), p. 70, describes the *Grecs du roi* cut by Garamond, 1544–50, as 'une nouvelle victoire du manuscrit sur le livre'. But they were only an improvement on those cut for Aldus fifty years before.

[2] A. Dain, *Les Manuscrits*, p. 69: 'La bâtarde, trop populaire, n'a pas resisté longtemps.'

[3] A. F. Johnson records his own observation of it in *French Sixteenth Century Printing* (London, 1928), p. 6.

[4] Beginning with his translation from J. B. Egnazio, *Summaire des chroniques* (Paris, 1529).

in adapting a lower case to them, and the result has no authority as a model for writing. In commending the antique letters Geoffroi Tory did not once mention the minuscules. He was intent on architecture and decoration: for him, and soon afterwards for everybody, Roman minuscules were printers' letters. The general adoption by printers of a kind of letter that could not be written without looking finicky and unnatural gave another blow to the illusion that printed books were written. Thenceforward printers' letters were judged by their suitability for reading and writing-masters' by their suitability for writing. Previously all types were 'script types', and it was the end of that state of affairs that opened the way for types that were 'script' in a new and special sense.

Granjon must have reconciled himself to the new function of a script type, for when it had become apparent that his *lettre françoise* would not win much acceptance for texts he went on cutting types of the same kind for a number of years.

In the Netherlands and in England the supersession of Gothic types for the northern languages came some thirty years later than it did in France, nor was it total. As in Germany Wolffgang Fugger in 1553 considered that 'it would not look well if German were to be set in Latin (Roman) letters',[1] so in Flanders in 1539 the grammarian Joos Lambrecht had to complain of the stubbornness of his countrymen in disliking anything but Gothic for the mother tongue.[2] For northern Europe it was momentous that Calvin with his French *Institution* of 1541 began a tradition of printing for the Reformed Church in Roman. The Geneva Bible weaned Englishmen of the Gothic onwards from 1560. The Dutch resisted Roman for Bibles but took to it for their own literature. Nevertheless, in England and in the Low Countries Black Letter was known as 'English', 'Duyts', and 'Vlaams' late in the seventeenth century and children were taught to read it first.[3] Sentiment in these countries clung to the formal Black and gave no justification for a Gothic cursive type.

---

[1] *Ein nutzlich und wolgegrundt Formular Manncherley schöner schrieften* (Nuremberg, 1553).   [2] *Refereynen int vroede, int zotte, int amoreuze* (Ghent, 1539).

[3] The order of the alphabets in Edmund Coote's *English Schoolemaster* as printed in the seventeenth century testifies to this in England. In the Netherlands it is expressly stated by D. A. Valcooch, *Den Regel der Duytsche Schoolmeesters* (Amsterdam, 1591), p. 26, and by the Bishop of Antwerp in 1619: V. de la Montagne, 'Schoolboeken te Antwerpen in de 17de eeuw', in *Tijdschrift voor Boek- en Bibliotheekwesen*, 5 (1907), pp. 3–35. The bishop's instructions on school books are discussed by M. Hoc in *Bibliotheca Belgica*, series III, fasc. 221, no. T 177, s.v. '*Tafel oft Liiste*', Antwerp, J. Cnobbaert, 1621. Cf. also R. Foncke, 'Schoolboeken te Mechelen in de 17de eeuw', in *Het Boek*, 15 (1926), pp. 263–8.

Civilité Types in France

The publication of Granjon's *Dialogue de la vie et de la mort* may be put at the end of 1557. No other printing in the same type is known to have been done in that year. The *Alexandreïs* of Gautier de Châtillon (6) dated from Granjon's press in 1558 is prefaced by a royal privilege given to him on 26 December 1557 forbidding for the space of ten years the cutting of punches or the use of type imitating his *lettre Françoise d'art de main*.[1] We know of nine books produced by Granjon in his first script type at Lyons in 1558, and five in 1559. In 1558 he sold a set of matrices for the type to Plantin, who printed a book (2) in it in the same year. Willem Silvius, also of Antwerp, had the type in 1562 (56), and Jean de Tournes at Lyons the year after (72). The use of this first Civilité type seems to have been limited to a very few printers, and of typefounders only one is known to have sold it[2]—and that was not until the eighteenth century.

The character of the books printed by Granjon in Civilité type in 1557–9 may give an idea of the light in which the types were regarded. We cannot tell whether they were deliberately chosen by him or his financial backers or literary advisers: they may have been the result of pure chance. They can be divided in three categories, *belles-lettres*, especially if translated from foreign languages, children's lesson-books, and songs set to music.

The first of these books, the *Dialogue*, gives such comfort to mortals as can be drawn from the pagan philosophers and the Scriptures (though not from the Sacraments or ministrations of the Church).[3] It was a successful publication: Granjon printed a second edition within a year (11),

---

[1] The material words are: 'Il ha pleu au Roy, nostre Sire, de donner priuilege et permission à Robert GranJon d'Imprimer ce p[rése]nt Livre (intitulé [etc.]) de sa lettre Francoise d'art de main: et pour remuneration de son Inuention, veult Iceluy Seigneur, que nul autre (quel qu'il soit) en ce Royaume: n'ayt à tailler poinssons, ne contrefaire lad[ite] lettre Francoise d'art de main. . . . Et ce pour le temps et terme de dix ans. . . .' What significance should be given to the expression 'd'art de main' is not clear. It may have a vague meaning, such as 'elaborated' or 'writing-master's'; or it may be a name given to the model that Granjon followed distinguishing it from the 'commune'.

[2] The only typefounder's specimen in which we have seen it was issued by Johann Pistorius at Basle in 1721 (reproduced, much reduced, in Albert Bruckner, *Schweizer Stempelschneider und Schriftgiesser* (Basle, 1943), facing p. 60. But that may mean that the Luther foundry at Frankfurt stocked it; for Pistorius equipped himself from there (ibid., pp. 59–60).

[3] The translator is named on the title-page as Jehan Louveau, rector of Chastillon de Dombes (near Lyons). He is said by Du Verdier to have been a native of Orleans (ed. Rigolet de Juvigny, Paris, 1772, iv, p. 453; and see E. and E. Haag, *La France protestante*, vii (Paris, 1835), pp. 138–9). He is credited with the translation of the pedagogical work by Otto Brunfels printed by Granjon in the next year, 1558. See p. 21.

and a third was published in 1562 (63). With Granjon's dedication to d'Urfé, setting forth his aims in cutting the type, it served as an advertisement to Frenchmen of the new script type. The *Alexandreïs* is a larger work (168 pages in quarto as compared with 90 in octavo) and clearly meant to bring the new typography to the notice of readers abroad. The writer of the foreword is careful to point out that it represents a style of handwriting common to Europe as a whole. The text is a medieval epic in Latin verse by Gautier de Châtillon (fl. 1170–80).[1] The use of the Civilité type for Latin possibly means that Granjon thought it proper for any printing done by Frenchmen, but there is evidence that the corresponding handwriting was thought suitable only for the vernacular.[2] Of the books printed in this style the *Joyeux Devis* of Des Periers (5) has by far the greatest reputation as literature, both for its own sake and for the influence of the author upon Rabelais. It is a collection of comic stories left unprinted at the author's death in 1544 and prepared for the press, so the preface tells us, by 'a certain virtuous person', supposedly Jacques Peletier.[3] In the same vein, though much inferior in style, are the *Facecies* of Domenichi which Granjon printed in 1559 with a French translation, a concession by Guillaume Rouillé, who held the privilege. The two books of verse by Berenger de la Tour in the manner of Ariosto (8, 9) and the late Greek anthology of legend translated by Gueroult (10) were humanistic *belles-lettres* of a minor order.

These books have been the quarry of great collectors, and they are worthy of their notoriety in the history of printing. Granjon set and printed them beautifully. Up to a point they reproduce the delightful patterns and rhythms of expert handwriting, a combination of neatness and verve needing only Granjon's admirable title-pages and fluent big initials to make ornamental books. Admittedly page after page set in these types can become tiresome: the repetition of a limited repertory of calligraphic flourishes is monotonous, and the attempt at freedom and variety cannot altogether prevail in a medium essentially mechanical. But it can do so up to a point; therefore it is hard to deny a great measure of success to the *Grecs du roi* or the Italics in the Roman Chancery manner or to any good Arabic type.

[1] F. J. E. Raby, *A History of Secular Latin Poetry in the Middle Ages*, ii (Oxford, 1934), pp. 72–82, 190.

[2] Apart from the normal practice of educated men of writing Latin and the northern languages in different scripts, there is the testimony of Granjon himself that the *lettre françoise* was 'propre seulement a nostre langue maternelle' (Foreword to the *Civilité puerile*, 1558).

[3] A. Tilley, *The Literature of the French Renaissance* (Cambridge, 1904), p. 131.

The school book that Granjon printed in 1558 has a particular interest because he added to the well-worn and generally accepted *Civilité puérile* of Erasmus a tract of a strongly Lutheran tendency. The title (reproduced as our frontispiece) announces it as 'La Discipline et institution des enfans, traduicte par Jehan Louueau'. The original was written in Latin by Otto Brunfels and published in 1525.[1] The Sorbonne condemned it in 1533, and the Index compiled by the university of Louvain in 1550 prohibited all the works of its author, a prominent follower of Luther. In disregarding these pronouncements Granjon was in the company of several printers at Lyons, Gryphius and De Tournes among them. This being Granjon's first book for children, he prefaced it with a recommendation of his type:

> So that youth aspiring to virtue and studying to acquire the manners suited to its years may have a twofold profit from this instruction in La Civilité puérile (gentle reader), I put it before you in the French character, proper only for our mother tongue believing that children may benefit not only from that instruction but from the letters too, as being the writing proper to their language and not borrowed from another people.

Children's lesson-books in Civilité type as vehicles for Protestant propaganda have lately been considered by Professor H. de la Fontaine Verwey,[2] who is able to cite several examples of the combination of instruction in writing with the elements of the reformed faith in books which, naturally, were condemned by Roman Catholic censors. A book of religious instruction for children was in the pack of every Protestant book-pedlar,[3] so the demand was constant.

Even though not meant to teach writing, the rudiments of religion for the young were often presented in Civilité. Granjon printed four booklets of the kind in 1562 (59–62). At that time the Reformers were active in this field of publishing, and given the close commercial relations of Lyons with Geneva,[4] Granjon may have hoped to develop

---

[1] This was established, so Le Coultre affirms, by J. W. Baum, in 'Notes sur l'impression dite de civilité et son inventeur', in 'Thesaurus Baumianus XLIX' (unpublished), pp. 233–7. The *De disciplina* had been printed at Strasbourg in 1540 without the passages most offensive to Catholics, see J. Le Coultre, *Maturin Cordier*, Neuchâtel, 1926, p. 87. We do not know whether Granjon included them.

[2] 'Typografische Schrijfboeken: een Hoofdstuk uit de Geschiedenis van de Civilité-letter', *De Gulden Passer*, 39 (1961), pp. 288–362.

[3] It was reported of a *colporteur* arrested in Savoy in 1556 that he was carrying 'les Bibles, Institutions chrétiennes, Instructions pour les petits enfants, Psaumes, et plusieurs autres ... imprimés à Geneve': C. L. Frossard, 'Berthelemy Hector, le colporteur martyr en 1556', in *Bulletin de la Soc. de l'hist. du Prot. français*, 31 (Paris, 1882), at p. 457.

[4] H. Chauvet, *Les Ouvriers du livre en France des origines à la Révolution de 1789*

a market there for evangelical books in script. He tried the market for
the Roman Catholic *Horae* in the same style (7), but his example was
very rarely followed.

Granjon cut at least three types for musical notation.[1] One of them
he equipped with notes of two kinds. Set with diamond-headed notes
it was suitable for psalms and could be used, according to the general
practice of the time, for measured music also; but he cut rounded notes
as an alternative and used them in scores for songs.[2] So set, the type
imitates handwriting, and the conjunction of it with Civilité for the
words is obviously appropriate. The scores for part-songs that Granjon
published in 1558–9 are very pretty indeed (Fig. 10).

Whether or not the privilege given to Granjon was meant to prevent
the use by other printers of type imitating the cursive French script,
a second type of the kind appeared at Paris in 1558 in books published
by Philippe Danfrie and Richard Breton. One of them, *Le Discours
de la court* (14), begins with a sonnet addressed by Danfrie to 'monsieur N. le Breton, secretaire de tresillustre et Reverendissime Cardinal
de Lorraine', describing the book as 'ma semence premiere' and
'premier coup d'essay', and opening with the lines:

> Récoignoissant que vous estes l'Autheur
> Que ceste lettre est produicte en lumiere . . .

And an inference that there had been an attempt to restrain the use of
the new type may be got from some verses prefacing *Les Divins oracles
de Zoroastre* issued by the same publishers, also in 1558 (15). The
author, François Habert, tells the reader:

> Outre cela tu verras à loisir
> (Dont receuras double contentement)
> Les traicts nouueaux d'une Françoise letre
> Que cy deuant Paris n'a sceu permettre
> Aux bons Esprits la voir aucunement.

On the face of it, it is paradoxical that one of the entourage of
the Cardinal Charles de Guise, a most determined persecutor of the

(Paris, 1959), pp. 215–18; E. Droz, 'Antoine Vincent, la propagande protestante par le
psautier', *Travaux d'humanisme et Renaissance*, 28 (Geneva, 1957), pp. 276–93.

[1] The punches for three which Plantin bought and ascribed to Granjon are kept
in the Museum Plantin-Moretus: 'Typographica Plantiniana II, Early Inventories of
Punches, Matrices and Moulds', *De Gulden Passer*, 38 (Antwerp, 1960), pp. 39, 58 (ST
64, 71a, 75). They include the one that Granjon used for the song-books of 1558–9
(ST 71a).

[2] Notes of the same shape had been cut earlier by Stephan Briard and printed in
Elzêar Genet, *Librum primum missarum Carpentras* (Avignon, Jean de Channay, 1532).
Those cut at Paris by Philippa Danfrie in 1559 and at Oxford by Peter de Walpergen
in 1694 are similar.

FIG. 9. A page of *Recueil de la diversité des habits*, Paris, R. Breton, 1562.
Type B1 and sand-cast [?] headline.

Huguenots, should have protected such an openly Protestant concern as Breton's press proved to be in the succeeding years. The memorial to Nicolas Le Breton formerly in the cathedral of Notre Dame, of which he was made a canon in 1559, indicates an expert in chancery business, therefore qualified to secure a dispensation from Granjon's exclusive privilege for the new type of Danfrie and Breton. He was one of the secretaries to the Colloques de Poissy in 1561 and later a prothonotary at Rome and secretary to Pius V.[1] He had dealings in property with Danfrie more than once.[2] In literary history he has gone down as a man who made trouble for Joachim du Bellay and was summed up, half-maliciously, in one of the poet's sonnets.[3] No privilege for the use of the new type is known to have been granted to Danfrie and Breton.

Philippe Danfrie was a fine metal-worker. He made astronomical and mathematical instruments and bookbinders' tools. In 1582 he was appointed 'Graveur général des monnaies de France', and at the time of his death in 1606 he was 'Valet de chambre' to Henri IV.[4] In a document of 1561, when he was some 25 years old, he was described as 'graveur en l'imprimerie'.[5] The inventory of the Le Bé typefoundry (c. 1598) attributed to Danfrie a 'Lettre françoise de Parengon' and a 'Musique des airs 16°', for which the foundry had matrices, and a 'Lettre françoise St. Augustin', for which it had the punches.[6] Two of Danfrie's types, imitating the 'lettre françoise' at a later stage of development, were made for a book that he wrote and published in 1597 on a kind of theodolite that he invented.[7] Prima facie one more Civilité type should be credited to him.[8]

---

[1] Émile Picot, 'Notices sur Nicholas Le Breton, Chanoine de Paris (1506–1574)', in *Bulletin de la Soc. de l'Histoire de Paris et de l'Île de France*, 31 (Paris, 1904), pp. 183–9.

[2] J. Pichon and G. Vicaire, *Documents pour servir à l'histoire des libraires de Paris, 1486–1600* (Paris, 1895), pp. 60–61.

[3] He has been identified with 'ung escrivain Breton que de ce temps la je tenois avec moi' (sc. at Rome) in a letter of Du Bellay (*Lettres de Joachim du Bellay*, ed. P. de Nolhac (Paris, 1883), p. 43) and with the subject of a sonnet in the *Regrets* (Paris, 1568), fol. 18ᵛ, for example in the introduction by E. Courbet to *Poésies latines et françaises de Joachim du Bellay* (Paris, 1919), p. xxxviii.

[4] F. Mazerolle, *Les Médailleurs français du XVᵉ siècle au milieu du XVIIIᵉ*, i (Paris, 1902), pp. lxxviii–lxxxi, Documents 208–24.

[5] Paris, Archives nat., S. 904, fol. 183. So also in 1565: J. Pichon and G. Vicaire, op. cit., p. 60.

[6] S. Morison, *L'Inventaire de la fonderie Le Bé* (Paris, 1959), pp. 21, 23, 25. Fournier le Jeune said the music was cut for Nicolas Duchemin: *Traité historique et critique sur l'origine et les progres des caractères de fonte pour l'impression de la musique* (Berne and Paris, 1765), p. 5.

[7] P. Danfrie, *Declaration de l'usage du graphometre* (Paris, 1597).   [8] See p. 29.

It seems, therefore, safe to assume that Danfrie cut the type in the books to which he put his name and that he took part in the venture with Breton in order to secure a return for his labour. Richard Breton had been printer and bookseller in Paris since 1551. He was born in 1524, the son of Guillaume Le Breton—perhaps, therefore, related to the Cardinal's secretary. He had to absent himself from Paris in 1563 because of his religious views,[1] therefore it is not surprising to find his publications avowedly Protestant.[2]

These partners printed wholly in Civilité, and, to judge by the prefatory matter in their earliest books, set much store by it as an attraction. Together they produced nine books in 1558–9,[3] but in the latter year six more appeared with the imprint of Breton alone.[4] Danfrie is found in another partnership for publishing in 1561. When Breton died in 1571 the punches and a set of matrices for two script types were inventoried among his goods.[5]

The texts of the books published by Danfrie and Breton and afterwards by Breton are set in a Civilité type on *St. Augustin* (English) body. Large initial letters and bold lines of lettering for titles are cut in wood and perhaps duplicated when necessary by castings in moulds of sand. The text type is not a copy of Granjon's *lettre françoise*: it is certainly made after another model, though news of Granjon's experiment may have led to its making. Being a little bigger than Granjon's first script, it is a little easier to read, and it is a fine piece of punchcutting albeit not quite the equal of Granjon's in verve and finish (Fig. 9). As for the genesis of this second Civilité type there is only the innuendo in the sonnet addressed by Danfrie to Nicolas Le Breton and printed before the *Discours de la court* (14) in 1558. From that it appears as though Le Breton wanted the type to be made and may have provided the model for it and that Danfrie thought he had 'carefully suited the *lettre françoise* to a great king of France'.[6] The significance of the allusion to the king is not obvious.

---

[1] Pichon and Vicaire, op. cit., p. 61.

[2] P. Renouard, 'Imprimeurs parisiens, libraires, fondeurs de caractères, et correcteurs d'imprimerie, depuis l'introduction de l'imprimerie à Paris (1470) jusqu'à la fin du XVIe siècle', in *Revue des bibliothèques*, 32 (1922), pp. 71–72.

[3] According to Jean de la Caille (*Histoire de l'imprimerie et de la librairie*, Paris, 1689, p. 41), Danfrie and Breton printed another book in 1558, Jacques Grévin's *Description du Beauvoisis*. We have not found a copy of it.

[4] G. Wildenstein, 'L'Imprimeur-libraire Richard Breton et son inventaire après décès', *Bibliothèque d'humanisme et Renaissance* 21 (1959), pp. 364–79.

[5] Paris, Arch. nat., Minutier central, Étude 122, liasse 129. See further p. 58.

[6] The sonnet, on sig. A2v of the *Discours de la court*, 1558, is as follows:

A Monsieur N. le Breton, Secretaire de tresillustre, et Reuerendissime Cardinal

Among the books published by Breton there was one of a Gallican and patriotic tendency for which the type might be thought appropriate. That was the *Devis de la langue francoise* by Abel Matthieu (25), a plea for a vernacular literature on a more popular level than that of Du Bellay. 'De toutes les Langues populaires et propres aux nations,' Matthieu wrote, 'la langue Francoise est la plus belle, la plus mignarde, et la mieux polie, si la langue Italienne ne l'egale. . . . Et quand nous escriuons, ou deuisons en Francois, il nous fault rapeller en la memoire les propres mots, les plus populaires, et les plus usez de la France.' The type was to some extent appropriate, too, for summaries and anthologies in French, and French translations, of the ancient historians and philosophers. However, most of Breton's books were religious or politico-religious; and it is difficult to avoid a conclusion that Civilité types were considered by many at that time to have some affinity with evangelism. Perhaps the familiar written hand added privacy to an appeal to the inmost conscience; certainly many converts were not much accustomed to read. However that may be, Breton published books so decidedly Protestant that it would be surprising if he sold them openly. A remarkable instance is the *Briefve instruction pour tous estats* (12, 29, 49), giving guidance in religion and morals to men of all conditions, and exhorting kings to govern themselves according to law.

Like Granjon's, Breton's publications in Civilité type resolve themselves into *belles-lettres*, Protestant piety, children's lessons, and music. He sponsored a new adaptation of the 'Civilité' of Erasmus by a Protestant author, Claude Hours de Calviac,[1] and a French version of the *Disticha* of pseudo-Cato (31, 111), a work which, in the original

de Lorraine, Philippe Danfrie, son treshumble seruiteur, desire perpetuelle félicité.

> Récoignoissant que vous estes l'Autheur
> Que ceste lettre est produicte en lumiere
> (Trescher Seigneur) la louange pleniere
> Vous en est deue, et suis vostre debteur.
> O des vertus et des arts Protecteur,
> Prenez en gré ma semence premiere,
> En bref aurez par facon singuliere
> De plus beaux traicts vn plus exquis labeur.
> Icy n'auez qu'un premier coup d'essay,
> Pour esprouuer ce que faire ie scay
> Dessous le pli de meilleur esperance.
> A tout le moins pour le commencement
>   Approprié J'ay curieusement
>   Lettre Francoise à un grand Roy de France.

[1] J. Le Coultre, *Maturin Cordier* (Neuchâtel, 1926), pp. 343–4.

Latin, revised by Erasmus and again by Maturin Cordier, was indispensable by the schools of Europe.[1]

Breton's printing of music is known by a single example, a selection from the odes of 'Anacreon' (22) put into French and set to music by

FIG. 10. Granjon's types for words and music in B. Beaulaigue, *Chansons nouvelles*, Lyons, R. Granjon, 1558. Type A1.

Richard Renvoysy, choirmaster of the royal chapel at Dijon.[2] The type for the music can hardly be other than a copy of Granjon's, with calligraphic notes of the same design. The volume dated in 1559 (fig. 11) has the imprint of Richard Breton alone, but it would be surprising if the music were not the one that Guillaume Le Bé attributed to Danfrie. It survived a long time in the house of Ballard, the king's printer of music, where it was known in 1765 as 'musique en copie par Philippe d'Anfrie'.[3] The expression 'copying music' must be taken to liken it to handwriting rather than the usual angular printer's type for the stave. It is a beautiful piece of work, more delicate and brilliant even than Granjon's. No mere coincidence could have made Breton's types for both words and music so like Granjon's.

[1] For the history of this book see Joseph Nève, *Catonis disticha* (Liège, 1926).
[2] G. Thibault, 'Un Recueil de musique imprimé en caractères de civilité par Richard Breton (1559)', in *Bibliothèque d'humanisme et Renaissance*, 2 (1935), pp. 302–8.
[3] Ibid., p. 304.

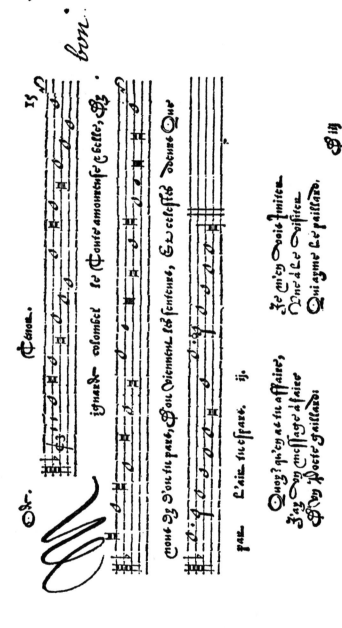

Fig. 11. Danfrie's Civilité and music types in *Quelques odes d'Anacreon mises en musique par . . . R. Renvoysy*, Paris, R. Breton, 1559. Type B1.

It must be said that Breton's printing in Civilité types was also of very high quality and his books are very attractive to the eye. Their only unsatisfactory features are large letters used for the main lines of titles, probably sand-cast in lines moulded from wooden patterns: they look clumsy beside the type (Fig. 31).

Danfrie's reputation as a letter-cutter is enhanced by another script type for a *lettre françoise* which we would attribute to him.[1] It occurs in some books published in Paris in 1561. One of them, the *Harangue de St Basile* (52), has Danfrie's name in the imprint with those of Jean Le Royer and Pierre Hamon. Le Royer had secured the appointment of King's Printer and Bookseller for Mathematics in 1554;[2] he was clearly in the partnership as printer. Hamon was a 'Secretaire de la Chambre du Roy' and a scribe, 'le plus renommé de France, voire de l'Europe, pour la perfection qu'il auoit d'escrire en toutes sortes de lettres'.[3] He, it must be supposed, designed the new type. Danfrie, the skilled metal-worker, can hardly have contributed to the joint stock anything but the punches. Two other books have some of the type of the *St Basile* in them: Hamon's book of models for handwriting, *L'Alphabet de linuention de lettres*, 1561 (51), with the imprint of Le Royer alone,[4] and an edition of Calvin's rudiments of Christianity for children of the same year (53). In Hamon's writing-book the *lettre françoise* is exemplified in many different cursive varieties. The models are engraved, but the new type is used for a prefatory sonnet by Ronsard claiming that the beauties of nature are excelled by Hamon's handwriting (Fig. 34). In a second edition, of 1566,[5] lacking the sonnet, a model is added for a 'lettre Palaceale', which is very much like the type of the *St Basile* (Fig. 35).

Plantin, who was in Paris in 1562–3, soon afterwards received the punches and a set of matrices and the mould for this face at Antwerp, and when he paid for a fount of it to be cast in 1564 he described it in his accounts as 'facon d'Escriture Inuention de Hamon'.[6] The punches (Fig. 15) are extant: they are admirably finished, and the face is perhaps

---

[1] See further, pp. 62–63.

[2] G. Lepreux, *Gallia typographica, Série parisienne*, vol. i, pt. 2 (Paris, 1911), Nos. 13, 22.

[3] *Premier volume de la bibliotheque du Sieur de la Croix du Maine* (Paris, 1584), quoted by A. Fairbank and B. Wolpe, *Renaissance Handwriting* (London, 1960), p. 77.

[4] *L'Alphabet de linuention des lettres en diuerses escritures* (Paris, J. Le Royer, 1561): BM 1268. a. 5.

[5] *Alphabet de plusieurs sortes de lettres par Pierre Hamon Blaesien Escrivain du Roy et Secretaire de sa Chambre* (Paris, 'Ils se vendent chez Robert Estienne, Imprimeur du Roy, 1567'): BN, Rés. pV. 104.

[6] Early Inv., p. 27.

the stateliest and the most elaborate of all that were made for Gothic script.

A premature end to the partnership for exploiting this type in France is only too likely, given the religious opinions of its members. Le Royer was faced with confiscation of his goods in 1562,[1] and Hamon was hanged in 1569.[2]

The activities of Granjon in the years 1559–62 are unknown, and the reasons for the lack of surviving books from his press during those years are open to conjecture. At that time the Psalms put into French by Clément Marot and Théodore de Bèze were printed in large numbers for sale in France. A bookseller from Lyons, Antoine Vincent, made his headquarters at Geneva in 1559, and from there organized the printing of the book.[3] The two editions in Granjon's script type by well-known printers at Geneva (38, 98) are examples of Vincent's enterprise.

By 1562 Granjon had nearly finished a second, bigger, type for the *lettre françoise* and had begun to print with it. Four little books of evangelical piety (59–62) bearing his imprint at Lyons in that year are set in a Civilité type on the body of *St Augustin* (English) lacking some of the capitals. The place of the missing letters is taken by the corresponding sorts of his first script. We have the authority of Plantin for ascribing the larger face to Granjon.[4] It is just as brilliant a piece of work as his first. The new type in the same unfinished state was used in a book (87) printed for Granjon at Antwerp in 1565 (Fig. 23), and we do not know of an example of it complete with all its proper capitals earlier than 1573 (135). Granjon used his new *St Augustin* script to launch the rudiments of grammar by Pierre Habert, *Le Moyen de promptement et facilement apprendre en lettre françoise, à bien lire, prononcer, et escrire*, to which he annexed *La Maniere de prier Dieu en toutes necessitez*.[5] A book in the same type in 1574 without a printer's

---

[1] Renouard, *Documents*, p. 93.

[2] E. and E. Haag, *La France protestante*, v (Paris, 1855), p. 424. There is doubt about his execution. See Elizabeth Armstrong, 'Deux notes sur Pierre Hamon', *Bibliothèque d'humanisme et Renaissance, Travaux et documents*, 25 (Geneva, 1963), pp. 543–51, at p. 551.

[3] E. Droz, 'Antoine Vincent, la propagande protestante par le psautier', in *Travaux d'humanisme et Renaissance*, 28 (Geneva, 1957), pp. 276–93.

[4] Early Inv., pp. 48–49.

[5] The book, with Granjon's imprint at Paris, in the Rue St Jean de Latran, à l'Arbre Sec, is undated. The *Catalogue* of the Bibliothèque Nationale gives it the date (1558). The evidence of the type is against a year much before 1574, when Aubert's *Hymne* (104) was printed in it with all the proper capitals. Granjon appears to have been living in Paris during 1573–4; in 1575 he let his house there (Baudrier, *Bibl. lyon.* ii, pp. 55–56).

name (137) may also be ascribed to Granjon's press, but by 1576 his second Civilité type was in use by others (148).

The decease of Richard Breton in 1571 marks the end of the attempt to introduce the *lettre françoise* as a type for texts of literary pretensions. In France thereafter its use was confined to children's lesson-books, if we except the house of De Tournes, where letters of the kind served for ornament and occasionally for distinction (165, 265).

An attempt without much consequence was made by Philippe Danfrie to bring typographic script into harmony with the progress of French current handwriting in 1597. His *Déclaration de l'usage du graphometre* published in that year (Fig. 36) is set in two faces cast on the body of Double Pica with one set of capitals for both (280). They are still *lettres françoises*, one *bâtarde*, the other *courante*, but they represent the native French handwriting at a stage of development later than the one imitated by Granjon, shorn of its flourish, tamed and rationalized, well on the way to becoming the *financière* of the eighteenth century. One other book in these types is known (363).

Evidently the rise and decline of Civilité types were linked to the fortunes of French Protestantism. They were at their height about the time of the Colloques de Poissy in 1560–1, when religious peace seemed a possibility and a good deal of licence was given to the profession and propagation of Huguenot principles. The Gallican trend that encouraged Granjon to bring the French script into printing entered also into religious politics on the side of independence of Rome. Here, as in Antwerp, publishers were strongly drawn to unorthodoxy by self-interest: a modern writer on French printers of the sixteenth century concludes that 'their biggest public was the French Protestant party; their best sellers were the books the French Reformed felt most necessary for their form of worship'.[1] As the tolerant phase passed and printers were increasingly troubled for their heterodoxy, from 1562 onwards, the use of the types by French printers became infrequent, and with the Massacre of St. Bartholomew in 1572 it ceased for a time. Association with the minority may have brought the types into disfavour with the Roman Catholic majority, and there is a gap of some ten years before they reappear in school books suitably expurgated or rewritten by orthodox pedagogues.

[1] R. M. Kingdon, 'The Business Activities of the Printers Henri and François Estienne', in *Travaux d'humanisme et Renaissance*, 28 (Geneva, 1957), at p. 275.

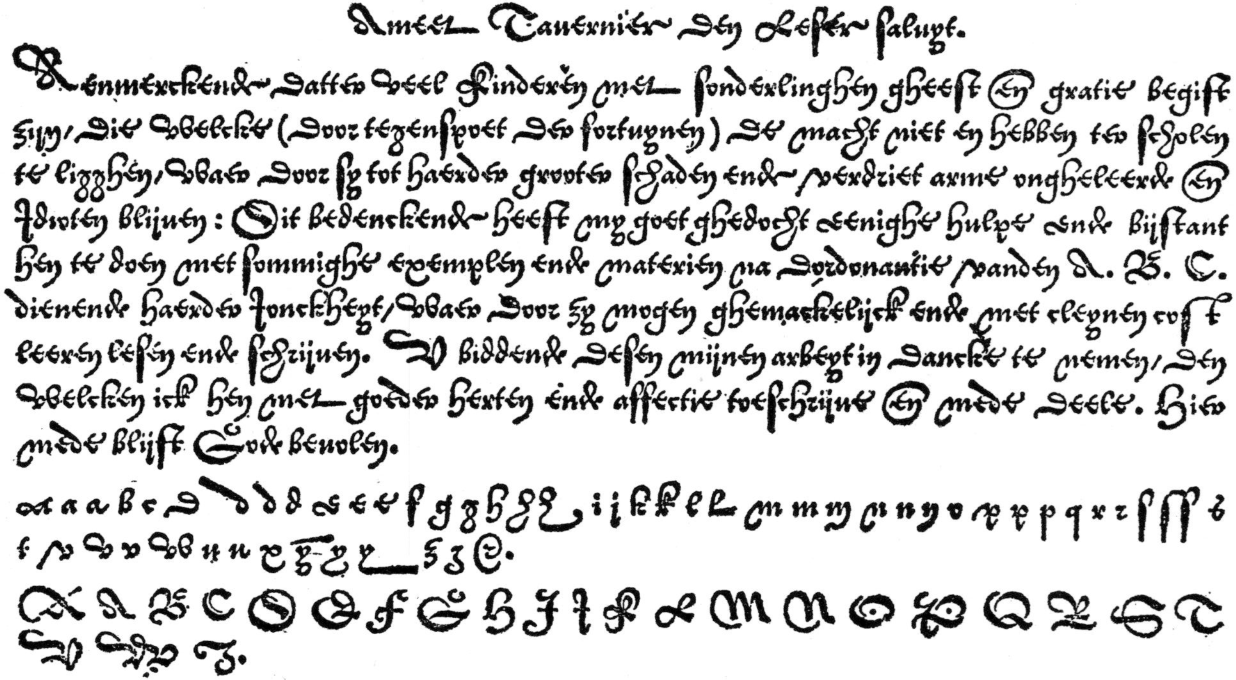

FIG. 12. The foreword to *Eenen gheestelycken ABC*, Antwerp, A. Tavernier, 1560. Type C1.

Civilité Types in the Netherlands

This style of printer's letter was eagerly accepted in the southern Netherlands. Plantin bought matrices for Granjon's *lectre faceon descriture* within a few months of its appearance in print. He used it for *A, B, C, ou instruction chrestienne pour les petits enfans* in 1558 (2). The author was 'Frère I. Pierre de Ravillan', probably a pseudonym, to whom was also attributed a different *Instruction chrestienne* printed at Plantin's press in 1562, as he said without his knowledge.[1]

The same type was bought by Willem Silvius, another enterprising and skilful printer at Antwerp.[2] He had it by 1562, when it appears in his edition of a play by Flemish rhetoricians performed at Antwerp (56).

The third Civilité type in order of date was cut by a Flemish craftsman, Ameet Tavernier, at Antwerp.[3] It is to be seen first in a version in Flemish of Erasmus *De Civilitate* entitled *Goede manierlijke seden*, printed, probably by Tavernier, at Antwerp in 1559 (17). This was put in the Roman Index of prohibited books of 1570, printed by Plantin. The type best fits a body of Double Pica, but Tavernier cast it on Paragon, which it overhangs slightly; it is, therefore, considerably bigger than the similar types previously made by Granjon and Danfrie. The Antwerp type is blacker, more rustic and Gothic in style, than the French, and no doubt an expert would find in it characteristics of the handwriting of the region (figs. 12, 37).

Tavernier's production of type imitating handwriting was celebrated in a ballad printed at Ghent in 1568,[4] where he is represented as unaware at the time of the pioneer enterprise of Granjon. In less than a year he had made a second such type, for *St Augustin* or English body, and this is found with the larger face in a book published at Antwerp in 1560 by Jean Bellere, *Le Tresor de la vertu* (37), and in the following years in several books with the imprint of Tavernier himself (45, 58, 69).

The Civilité types found a wider use in the Low Countries than they did in France. Until they were superseded by script types rendering the round hand in the middle of the eighteenth century, many Dutch and Flemish printers stocked them. They served for jobbing of various

[1] Max Rooses, *Le Musée Plantin-Moretus, contenant la vie et l'œuvre de Christophe Plantin et de ses successeurs, les Moretus* (Antwerp, 1914), pp. 22, 32.

[2] Colin Clair, 'Willem Silvius', *The Library*, 5th ser., 14 (1959), pp. 192–205.

[3] M. Parker, K. Melis, H. D. L. Vervliet, 'Typographica Plantiniana III. Ameet Tavernier, punchcutter, ca. 1520–1570', *De Gulden Passer*, 39 (1961), pp. 17–76.

[4] Marcus van Vaernewyck, *Spieghel der Nederlandscher audtheydt* (Ghent, 1568), Book iv, fol. 141.

kinds and in a minor role for bookwork. Certain Dutch works of piety or courtesy and of instruction for the young were set at least partly in Civilité type well into the nineteenth century; but the works chosen for this treatment were not many and they were aimed at a humble kind of reader. There was no vernacular Dutch literature of the highest aims when these types were introduced, for the men capable of writing it were still obliged to express themselves in Latin in order to reach a numerous public. So the language was associated with a homely kind of religious and moral instruction, with folk tales, and with books for the young. For these the Civilité types were appreciated, the readers being bred to reading Black Letter and writing a Gothic cursive. For the same reason many edicts, notices, and forms issuing from the central and local governments in the Netherlands, when written in Dutch, were set in the script types as soon as these were available, and publishers of news-pamphlets liked them for quoted matter.

Under Spanish rule censorship was incapable of preventing the printing and circulation of a fair volume of tracts favouring the reformers in religion. The city authorities of Antwerp were reluctant to enforce the Spaniards' strict regulations for the book-trade for fear of offending the foreign merchants on whom their prosperity depended. Here, as in France, children's books set in Civilité types were often meant to teach Protestantism as well as handwriting.[1] Plantin's *A B C ou instruction chrestienne* was reprinted by him in 1564 with the *Civilité puérile* and the *Discipline et instruction des enfans* by Brunfels (76). Ameet Tavernier about 1561–3 (36) and Silvius in 1564 printed *Eenen gheestelijken A B C* (81) (fig. 12) which the Roman censors put on their Index of 1570. *Eenen nieuwen A B C* by Dirk Coornhert, published by Silvius in 1564 (fig. 22), 1567, and 1568 (80, 103, 118), is suspect of irreligious hedonism. All these were in script types.

Silvius seems to have kept in particularly close touch with Granjon, and being himself an accomplished calligrapher,[2] he favoured calligraphic types. He had a fount of Civilité compounded of two faces by Granjon with some special characters to be seen only in his printing;[3] he was the first customer for the second, the *St Augustin*, script by Granjon, which he used in its unfinished state in 1565 for an edition shared with the punchcutter;[4] and in that year he began using a larger, somewhat condensed and semi-cursive *lettre françoise*, so closely re-

---

[1] These are dealt with fully by H. de la Fontaine Verwey in his article, previously cited, on 'Typografische Schrijfboeken', to which we owe much of our information.

[2] His model for Italic is reproduced in his edition of *Eenen nieuwen A B C* (80).

[3] See below, p. 48.

[4] Nos. 87 and 90 in our list.

sembling a type cut later by Granjon as to leave little doubt that he made it.[1] No other printer is known to have had this type (fig. 24), which had no capitals and appears to have been experimental. And then, in 1566 (94), Silvius added to his equipment a very fine new Civilité type on the body of *St Augustin* (fig. 25), so expertly cut and so accomplished in style as to be attributable, though conjecturally, only to Granjon. Thenceforward it was the only script type to be seen in the work of Silvius, and he was the only printer to use it until his death at Leyden in 1580 and the sale of his material by his son two years later, when it became available to other printers in Holland.[2]

Granjon must in the years 1563–70 have spent much of his time in Antwerp, to judge by the records of him in the accounts kept by Plantin. The account-books (fig. 1) show that in 1566–7 Plantin bought from Granjon the punches and sets of matrices for three previously unknown *lettres françoises*, one described as 'cut lately in this city'.[3] Two of them were types for large-bodied letters imitating scripts more formal than the 'commune courante' and meant, as seems likely, for headings and emphasized matter in texts set in the smaller and more cursive letters (fig. 27). One of them, named 'Courante' by Plantin,[4] is a more regular and careful cutting of the letters that Silvius had used the year before. The other was an up-to-date writing-master's *bâtarde*, and by that name Plantin knew it. A single set of capitals, punctuation, and figures did for both, and the capitals differ not at all in form from those made for the smaller Civilité types. The third of Plantin's purchases was an incomplete set of punches and matrices for a *lettre françoise* on the small body of Garamond (Long Primer), the smallest for which this kind of letter was cut. It was never put to any use.

By buying the punches for the Courante and Bastarde Plantin made sure of having the types to himself during his lifetime, ending in 1589. To that there was an exception: Jean de Tournes II had the Bastarde by 1578 (165). The explanation lay probably in a term in the contract with Plantin allowing Granjon to keep a set of matrices for his own use and the disposal of his set to De Tournes. This particular contract has not survived, but other contracts between the same parties have this term. De Tournes had the Courante also some years later (290). After Plantin's death the matrices for the two big *lettres françoises*

[1] We name it 'Pré-Courante' because of its likeness to the Courante. See pp. 48–49.
[2] We call this the 'Dutch *St Augustin*'. See p. 51. [3] Early Inv., p. 38.
[4] It is hard to explain this name for the type, because it represents a hand less current than the *françoises* cut before it.

were in his office at Leyden and the type served for some of the books printed there by Raphelengius. Some Dutch typefounder appears to have come by them afterwards, for founts of the Bastarde were not uncommon in Holland for a time, and after their disappearance the design was copied by an unidentified punchcutter, presumably in Holland.[1]

There could have been no better way for a punchcutter of the latter part of the sixteenth century to advertise his competence than by having a Civilité face to his credit. Perhaps for this reason Hendrik van den Keere of Ghent cut a *Mediaan geschreven* (Pica script) (fig. 39) which is remarkable for its minute elegance and neatness. It is to be found first in 1571 in a book printed at Louvain (129*a*) and a year later in one from Antwerp (130). Not long before Van den Keere died in 1580, Jan van Hout, the town clerk of Leyden, equipped his press in the Raedhuys with this type to set the town's charters and ordinances. It is not surprising, though, that he found it 'much too small and too sharp' for his big, solid pages and broadsides and had to replace it largely by Granjon's bigger and blacker Bastarde.[2]

Men with less skill, such as the typefounders named Van Wolsschaten of Antwerp, produced types of the same description (fig. 40) late in the sixteenth century and in the first quarter of the next. Some of them were content to put together matrices of various origins producing letters of different sizes and styles, so that types of distinct appearance may have little or no real novelty about them. However, about 1768 Matthieu Rosart of Brussels cut a complete new Civilité face (fig. 44). It was long after 1800 that Dutch and Flemish children ceased to learn the rudiments of their mother tongue in these types and older people to derive comfort from such pious works as 'The testament of Lowys Porquin' and 'The Four Last Things', or reluctant letter-writers to model themselves on manuals for family correspondence presented in the conventional script.

Civilité Types in Great Britain

If we may judge by surviving examples, Scotland was five years ahead of the south in bringing this hand into printing; for Thomas Bassandyne of Edinburgh had a fount of Granjon's first script type by 1571. In that year he printed Robert Henryson's adaptation of Aesop,

---

[1] For this 'Enschedé's bâtarde' see below, p. 85.

[2] W. I. C. Rammelman Elsevier, 'De voormalige Drukkerij op het Raadhuis der Stadt Leyden, 1577–1610', in *Nieuwe Reeks van Werken van de Maatschappij der Nederlandsche Letterkunde te Leiden*, 10 (1857), pp. 282–5.

Morall Fabillis, in it (129). Bassandyne and, later, Thomas Finlason set a few official notices (140, 326) in this type, but no other book that has come to light.[1]

In England these types were used almost exclusively to simulate engrossing. It is true that the earliest recorded occurrence of a Secretary type in this country is in a book, Guarna's *Bellum grammaticale* (*the Grammer Warre*), printed in 1576 by Henry Bynneman (146);

SECRETARY.

Great Primer.

Byddel 10.   Matrices 114.

FIG. 13. Great Primer Secretary type in *A Catalogue and Specimen of the Printing-Type Foundery of Mr. John James*, 1782. Type H2. See also fig. 46.

but its function there was only to set the colophon, and for that purpose it was manifestly too big. This first English type of the Civilité class was a face for Great Primer body in style akin to the Flemish and quite as well cut (figs. 13, 46). It has a capital C of the old, closed form (⊕) and ligatures of sh and ld, suggesting that it was made for setting English; moreover the letters conform generally with the models for the *litera anglicana* by Martin and Bales in the *Theatrum artis scribendi* of Judocus Hondius (Leyden, 1594). The skilful cutting of the letters and the poor justification of the matrices might be an indication that the punches were imported and struck in London. There is no reason to think the type was ever used outside England, and here it is found only in the book previously cited from Bynneman's press and later in jobs attributable to the King's Printing House. 'One mattris of secritary xls.' is an item in the inventory of Bynneman's

---

[1] A. F. Johnson, *Type Designs, their History and Development*, 2nd ed. (1959), p. 141. Dr. William Beattie has kindly told us of the use of the type in another book by Bassandyne, *The CL Psalms of David* (Edinburgh, 1575), to give directions for the melodies.

goods made after his death in 1583.[1] Thereafter for some thirty years it is found in official notices and forms, among them vintners' licences and victuallers' recognizances,[2] demands for taxes by King James I, and a proclamation of 1593 about the measurement of timber.[3] Bynneman owned not only matrices for the type but 'lettres cut in wood for the secritarie xii', that is to say big initials to go with it. Surely he must have used them, but we find no trace of them until he was dead and they occur with the Secretary in jobbing work.

It is hard to tell how far our ignorance of early English printing in Civilité types may be due to destruction of the subject-matter. There is no trace of an 'A.B.C. imitating handwriting' produced in London in 1570, according to a contemporary record;[4] and the *Short-Title Catalogue* can muster only an absurdly small remnant of the *A.B.C.* in any form. John Day had the monopoly of it with the Catechism in English, and Reginald Wolfe in Latin, since 1552; the one's son and the other's widow ceded their rights to the Stationers' Company. The Company stopped the printing of other books teaching the alphabet, such as *The pathway to learne to write & Read wrytten hand* and *The book of graces with the A.B.C.* in 1601.[5] The monopoly, regranted in perpetuity in 1603, made it unnecessary for the grantees to invest in special types to lend added appeal to the rudiments of grammar. The Secretary hand was part of an English elementary education until near the end of the seventeenth century; but in earlier years models were written,[6] perhaps sometimes engraved. Engraved specimens of Secretary are found in the editions of 1627 and 1630 of Edmund Coote's *English Schoolemaster*, first published in 1597.

The lack of an English version of Erasmus on *Civilitas morum puerilium* printed after 1554 is in itself remarkable,[7] and it meant that no English printer was tempted to follow the French fashion of setting it.

---

[1] Mark Eccles, 'Bynneman's Books', in *The Library*, 5th ser., 12 (1957), pp. 81–92, at p. 84.

[2] H. Jenkinson, 'English Current Writing and Early Printing', *Transactions of the Bibliographical Society*, 13 (1916), pp. 273–95, at pp. 291–2.

[3] We can add nothing to the account of the subject by Mr. A. F. Johnson in the book referred to above, pp. 140–45.

[4] Colin Clair, in *The Library*, 5th ser., 14 (1959), at p. 195.

[5] *Records of the Court of the Stationers' Company 1576 to 1602*, ed. W. W. Greg and E. Boswell (1930), pp. 75, 83.

[6] John Brindley, *Ludus literarius, or the Grammar Schoole* (1612), p. 31.

[7] The precepts are digested and versified in G. D.'s *Directions for Writing* (1656, reprinted privately, Cambridge, 1933). *The Rules of Civility, or Certain Ways of Deportment observed in France* (1671 and later), translated from a work by Antoine de Courtin, is for adults and quite different.

A second English Secretary type introduced in the early years of the seventeenth century was used mainly for law forms.[1] It represents a slow and ceremonious hand in which certain letters even have serifs at the feet: it lacks altogether the cursive quality which made earlier Civilité types attractive to the eye, and some of its capitals are uncouth (fig. 53). Law printers used it for personal bonds and powers of attorney and the forms, such as marriage licences and letters of administration on intestacy, issuing from the ecclesiastical chanceries. It went out of use not long before 1700. This type served for the model in the appendix to the *English Schoolemaster* when it was printed in 1636 (374), and in several later editions (394–6, 398). The origin of this second type is unknown.

A third English type of the kind (fig. 54) is known only by its appearance in John Barnard's handsome *Book of Selected Church Musick*, printed in London in 1641 (376). It is like the second in the formation of the letters, and looks as though it might have been cut by the same man.

Secretary handwriting persisted in England for engrossing legal documents long after it had ceased to be used for business; and about 1765 Thomas Cottrell issued a specimen of his 'New Printing type in imitation of the Law Hand',[2] showing a character still Gothic though influenced by the modern round hand (fig. 43).

A Type for German Current Hand

We have not included German types in our survey, for those made in imitation of Gothic scripts are in general quite different in style from any to which the name 'Civilité' has been applied. Most of the German script types were cut after the middle of the seventeenth century, by which time the national handwriting had diverged widely from the French and Dutch. In the sixteenth century, however, Germans wrote a *Current Schrift* which was very like the *lettre françoise* or the English Secretary,[3] and while they did so a type was made to represent their *gemein*, *gelegt* upright hand as it is shown, for example, in the manuals of Johann Neudörffer (1538) and Wolffgang Fugger (1553).[3] It was used by Christoph Froschauer the younger of Zurich for passages in a book by Hans Blum, *Ein kunstrych Buch von allerley antiquiteten*,

[1] A. F. Johnson, *Type Designs*, p. 143.
[2] Berry and Johnson, p. 34.
[3] See *Johann Neudörffer d. Ä., der grosse Schreibmeister der deutschen Renaissance*, introduced by Albert Kapr (Leipzig, 1956); *Wolfgang Fuggers Schreibbüchlein: vollständige Faksimile-Ausgabe des 1553 in Nürnberg erschienenen Werkes*, introduced by Fritz Funke (Leipzig, 1958).

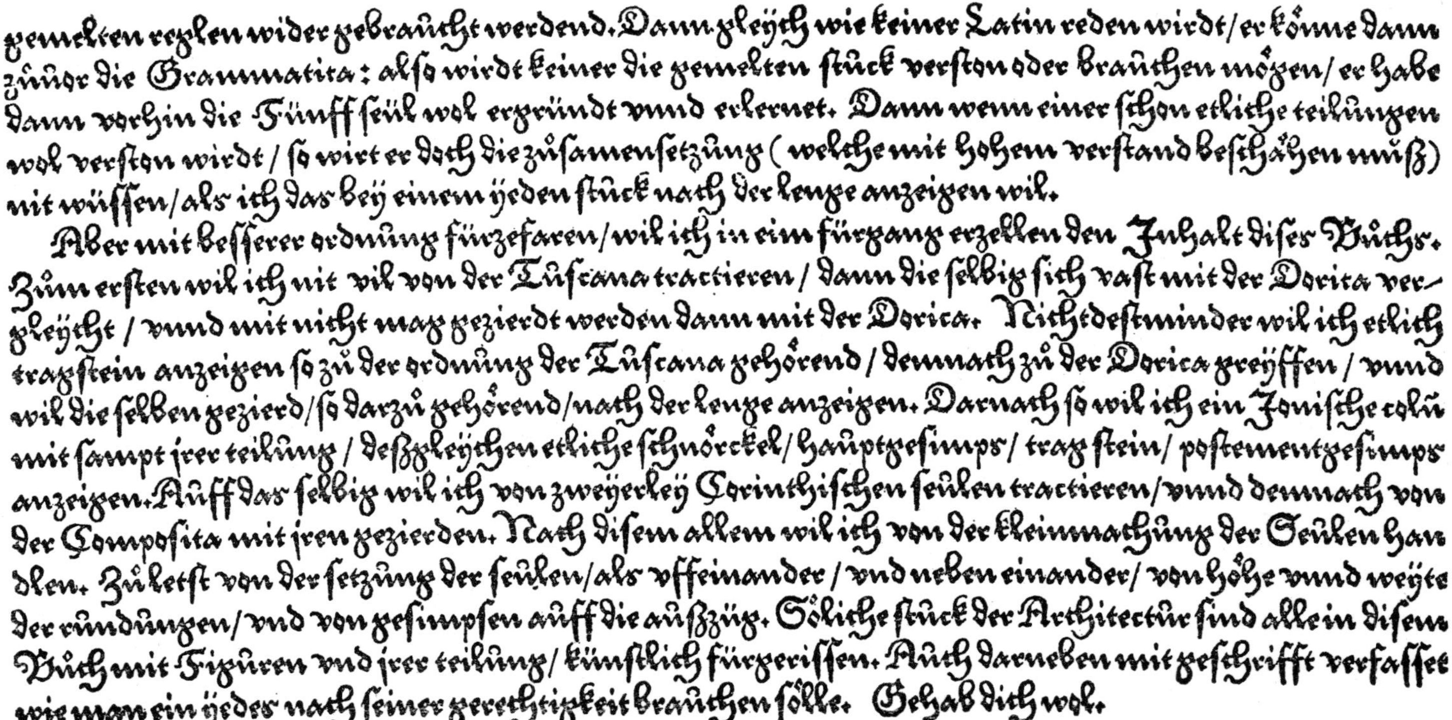

gemelten reglen wider gebraucht werdend. Dann gleych wie keiner Latin reden wirdt/ er kōme dann
zůuor die Grammatica: alſo wirdt keiner die gemelten ſtuck verſton oder brauchen mögen/ er habe
dann vorhin die Fünff ſeül wol ergründt vnnd erlernet. Dann wenn einer ſchon etliche teilungen
wol verſton wirdt/ ſo wirt er doch die zůſamenſetzung (welche mit hohem verſtand beſchähen můß)
nit wüſſen/ als ich das bey einem yeden ſtuck nach der lenge anzeigen wil.

Aber mit beſſerer ordnung fürzefaren/ wil ich in eim fürgang erzellen den Inhalt diſer Bůchs.
Zům erſten wil ich nit vil von der Tůſcana tractieren/ dann die ſelbig ſich vaſt mit der Dorica ver-
gleycht/ vnnd mit nicht mag geziert werden dann mit der Dorica. Nichtdeſtminder wil ich etlich
tragſtein anzeigen ſo zů der ordnung der Tůſcana gehörend/ demnach zů der Dorica greyffen/ vnnd
wil die ſelben gezierd/ ſo darzů gehörend/ nach der lenge anzeigen. Darnach ſo wil ich ein Joniſche colū
mit ſampt irer teilung/ deßgleychen etliche ſchnörckel/ hauptgeſimps/ tragſtein/ poſtementgeſimps
anzeigen. Auff das ſelbig wil ich von zweyerley Corinthiſchen ſeülen tractieren/ vnnd demnach von
der Compoſita mit iren gezierden. Nach diſem allem wil ich von der kleinmachung der Seülen han
dlen. Zůletſt von der ſetzung der ſeülen/ als vffeinander/ vnd neben einander/ von höhe vnnd weyte
der ründungen/ vnd von geſimpſen auff die außzüg. Söliche ſtuck der Architectur ſind allein diſem
Bůch mit Figuren vnd irer teilung/ künſtlich fürgeriſſen. Auch darneben mit geſchrifft verfaſſet
wie man ein yeder nach ſeiner gerechtigkeit brauchen ſölle. Gehab dich wol.

FIG. 14. German script type in Hans Blum, *Ein kunstrych Buch*, Zurich, 1567.

in 1567 (fig. 14).[1] The German writing and the type are unlike the
Secretary hands in more westerly countries in having oblique, back-
ward-leaning, instead of upright, mainstrokes, and the type adopts the
simplest and least cursive of the many permissible forms for the
capitals, virtually those of the *Fraktur*. Certain of the minuscules in
Froschauer's fount have peculiarly German forms, g k p and final s,
far removed from the French but very close to some used in the
Netherlands and Great Britain. The general effect, however, is of a
Civilité type; and the face makes an interesting comparison with the
rest of the class because it shows that the Flemish types represent a
cross between the French and the German in the drawing of the
letters and the thickness of the strokes.[2]

[1] Part of a page is reproduced by D. B. Updike, *Printing Types, their History, Forms,
and Use*, 3rd ed. (Cambridge (U.S.A.) and London, 1962, vol. i, fig. 77. The elder
Froschauer had this type by 1560: Paul Leeman-van Elck, *Die Offizin Froschauer*
(Zurich and Leipzig, 1940), p. 167.

[2] For other German script types, see A. F. Johnson, *Type Designs*, pp. 136–8.

III

DESCRIPTIONS OF THE TYPES AND
HISTORIES OF THE MATERIAL FOR
CASTING THEM

A. GOTHIC SCRIPT TYPES BY ROBERT GRANJON

A1. *The Cicéro lettre françoise* (figs. 7, 8, 10, 17, 18)

For this, the earliest of the Civilité types, Plantin owned a set of finished matrices and a strike. He used the type for an *A.B.C.* in 1558 (2), only a few months after its first use by Granjon himself at Lyons. In his Inventory of 1563 Plantin entered 'Mediane faceon dEscriture a la main Granion contenant 138 matrices' and (under 'Matrices non-Justifiees') 'Lectre francoyse de Granjon grandeur du Median'. *Mediaan* is Dutch for 'Pica'.

The two sets are still at the Museum Plantin-Moretus. There is no record of the purchase. Nothing is known about the history of the punches, which Granjon, presumably, kept. For some time past, as an old label on the box shows, the number of the justified matrices has been 135, the capitals X Y Z being absent. They are for 21 capitals, 53 single lower-case letters, 31 ligatures, 14 accented letters, and 7 punctuation-marks. With these are 9 unjustified matrices. The strike is of only 103 pieces. Plantin used the type often (2, 35, 44, 76, 79). Willem Silvius, also of Antwerp, published books set in this face in 1562 (56) and 1568 (118).

Another set of matrices probably belonged to Jean de Tournes and to his son, the second of the name. The type appears in books from their press from 1563 (72) until 1619 (351), the press being by then in Geneva, where this face was in use as early as 1561 (48). In 1721 Johann Pistorius, a typefounder at Basle, showed it in a specimen of the types that he sold (437). Unlike the other script types by Granjon, this was not in the inventory of the Le Bé foundry at Paris or in the specimen-book of Delacolonge at Lyons in 1773.

The Widow Ewouts had the type at Amsterdam by 1567 (99), and other printers there after her (206, 207, 232, 233); but no Dutch typefounder is known to have stocked it.

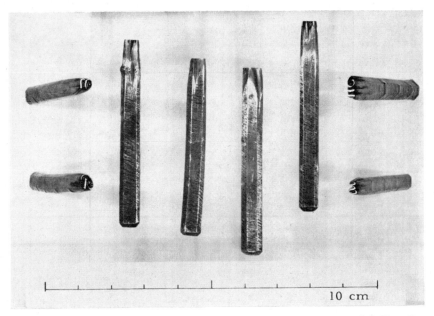

FIG. 15. Punches for the *Petite Augustine françoise*, probably cut by Danfrie. Type B3

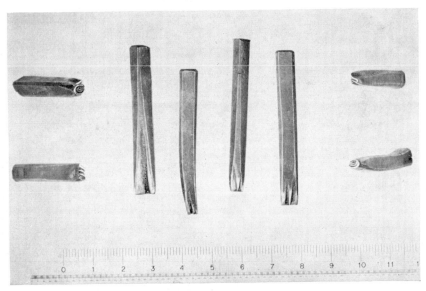

FIG. 16. Punches for the *St. Augustin* Civilité type of R. Breton, probably cut by Danfrie.
Type B1

F𝐈𝐆. 17. Matrices at the Museum Plantin-Moretus for the *Cicéro lettre françoise* of Granjon. Type A1

For his *Horae* of 1558 (7) Granjon cast this face on a body of Small Pica or *Philosophie* (fig. 8).

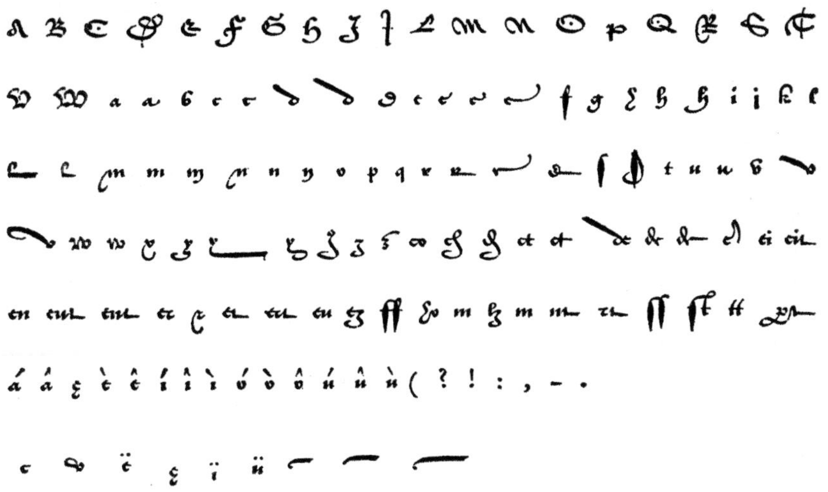

FIG. 18. The characters of the *Cicéro lettre françoise* of Granjon cast in matrices at the Museum Plantin-Moretus. Type A1.

A2. *The St Augustin lettre françoise of Granjon* (figs. 19, 21)

Four tracts with Granjon's imprint at Lyons in 1562 are the earliest examples of composition in his second script type, though in an unfinished state, lacking some of the capitals. It was a bigger face than the first, and though it was called *St Augustin* (English), it needed a body rather more than that. Plantin listed it under 'Augustine grosse'.[1] Still in its unfinished state, it served for an edition printed by Willem Silvius for himself and Granjon in 1565 (87, 90). Complete with all the proper capitals it is found in a book with Granjon's imprint at Paris, undated but with an address at a house that he occupied in 1573–4.[2]

The first or the second Guillaume Le Bé acquired 143 matrices for this face before the inventory of their typefoundry was drawn up about 1598,[3] so that founts were generally available in France. Another set of matrices, perhaps one that Granjon made for himself, remained at Lyons and belonged in 1773 to Delacolonge, typefounder of that

[1] Early Inv., p. 71.

[2] No. 135 in our list. The foreword is dated in 1558, therefore there may have been an earlier edition. For Granjon's house in Paris, see Baudrier, *Bibliographie lyonnaise*, sér. 2, p. 54.

[3] S. Morison, *L'Inventaire de la fonderie Le Bé*, p. 21.

city (518). Delacolonge recut the long f and showed the face as 'Civilité de Cicero', cast on a Pica body.

Plantin acquired a strike and sent it in 1578 to be justified;[1] he had begun using the type by 1580 (194). His matrices, originally 125, have dwindled to 76 since they were entered in an inventory of 1652.

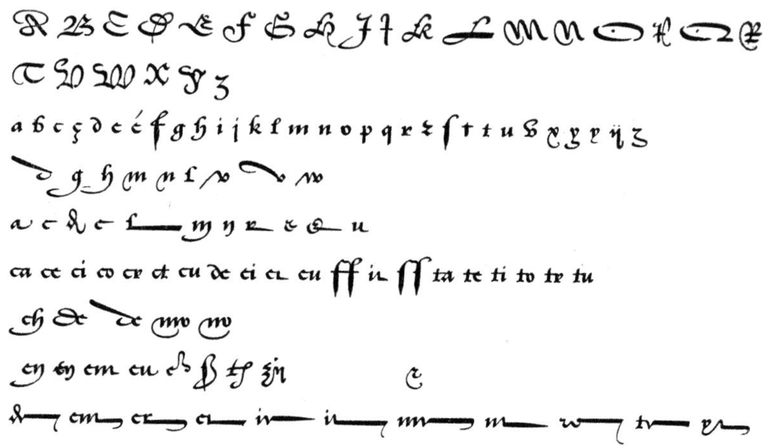

FIG. 19. The characters of the *St Augustin lettre françoise* of Granjon cast in matrices belonging to Messrs. Joh. Enschedé en Zonen. Type A2.

Messrs. Enschedé have a better-preserved set of matrices, 130 in all (their No. 11), and trace its ascent to Hermanus Uytwerf, a printer and typefounder at Amsterdam in the early part of the eighteenth century.[2] This set is made up of 25 capitals, 52 single lower-case letters, and 43 ligatures.

One of the matrices in the set owned by Enschedé is for ligatured *zij*, a combination that could be used only for setting Dutch (or Flemish). Granjon must have cut the face while he was working in close contact with printers in the Netherlands.

This was the favourite Civilité type. In it were set most of the interminable series of lesson-books, the *Civilité puérile*, the *Quatrains de Pybrac*, the *Distiques de Caton*, beginning in the later years of the sixteenth century and ending only after three hundred years. In 1858 Louis Perrin revived it for a book of verse,[3] and so did Enschedé en Zonen for *Les Œuvres de Louise Labé* in 1871.[4]

---

[1] Early Inv., p. 79.   [2] Enschedé, *Fonderies*, p. 47.
[3] Joséphin Soulary, *Sonnets humoristiques*, illustrated by Sabbe and Audin, fig. 29.
[4] *The House of Enschedé*, Haarlem, 1953, p. lv.

It is deservedly a famous type. If Granjon did not do noticeably better the second time, as he promised that he would in his dedication in 1557,[1] he made a type that was better proportioned to the average

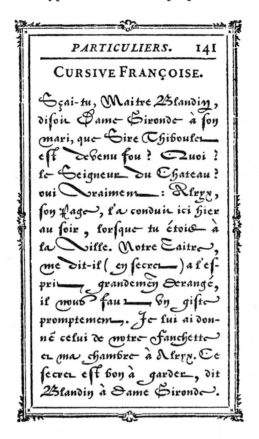

FIG. 20. The specimen of 'Cursive françoise' in the *Manuel typographique* of Fournier le Jeune (vol. ii, 1766). Type A2+B1 (a mixture of Granjon's and Breton's *St Augustin*). There are several literal errors.

page. Among the modifications made to his earlier design are wider forms for L O Q, and these are better proportioned to the alphabet as a whole.

Some typefounders evidently had defective sets of matrices for Granjon's *St Augustin* and eked them out with sorts taken from other Civilité types. The specimen of the 'Cursive françoise' (our fig. 20) in the second volume of the *Manuel typographique* of Fournier le jeune (1766) is compounded of sorts taken from this type by Granjon and some from the *St Augustin* of Danfrie and Breton (our B1). The

[1] See above, p. 11.

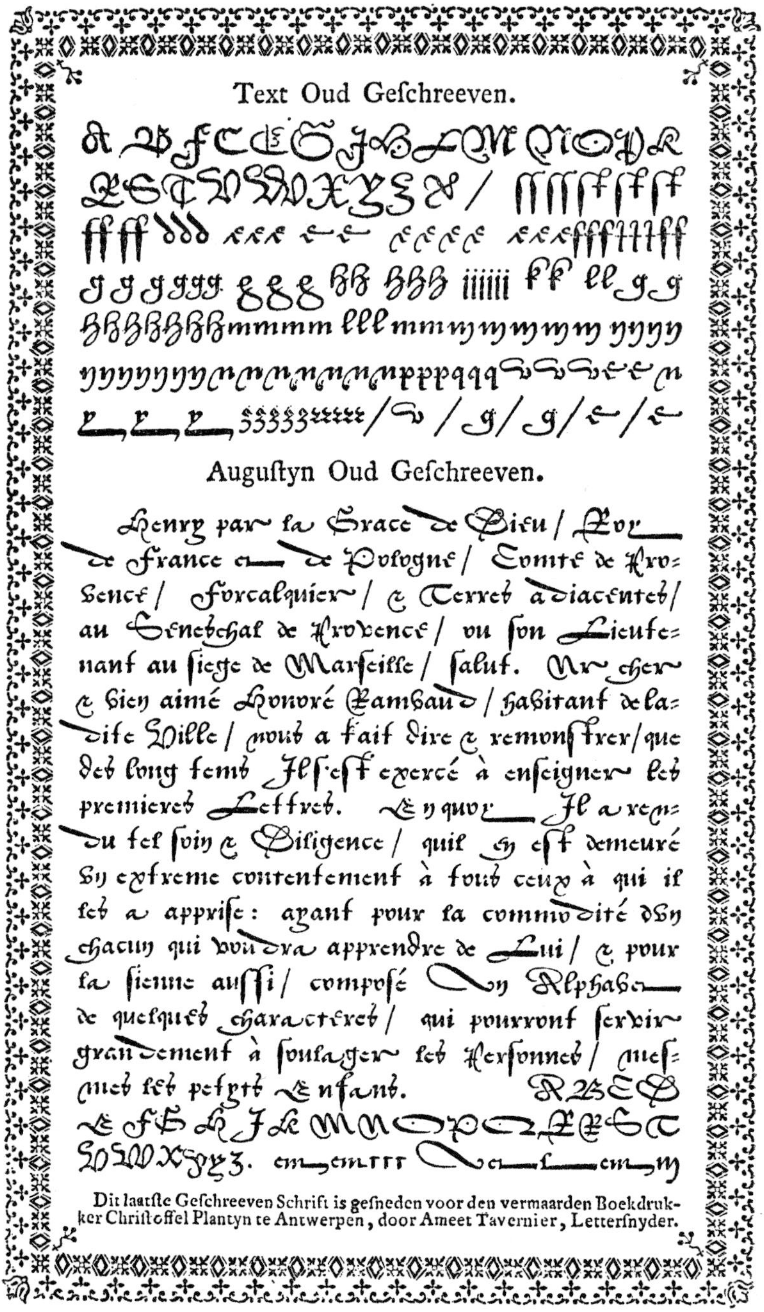

Auguftyn Oud Gefchreeven.

(specimen of Civilité types in ornamental script)

Dit laatfte Gefchreeven Schrift is gefneden voor den vermaarden Boekdruk-
ker Chriftoffel Plantyn te Antwerpen, door Ameet Tavernier, Letterfnyder.

FIG. 21. The specimen of Civilité types in the *Proef van Letteren* of Johannes
Enschedé (see p. 81). The smaller is mainly Granjon's *St Augustin*.

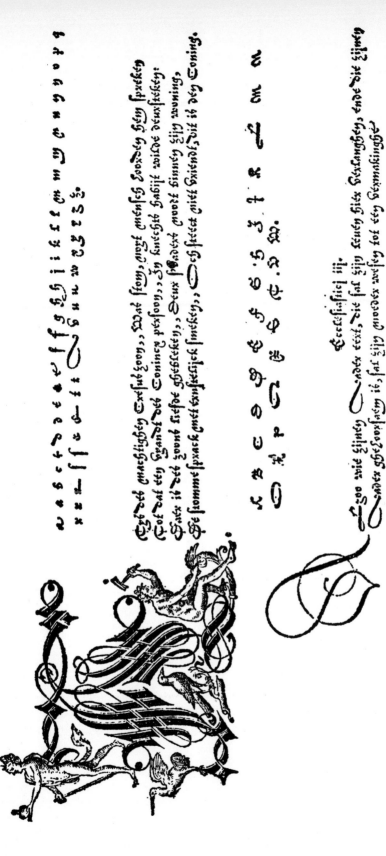

Fig. 22. A page of *Eenen nieuwen A B C*, Antwerp, W. Silvius, 1564. Type Aza. Granjon's *St Augustin* mixed with his *Cicéro* and A E K c d e r specially cut for Silvius.

same blend is found afterwards in many French books: in fact in the nineteenth century it was the commonest Civilité type in France. On the other hand, in Antwerp for a spell in 1592–3 defects in a fount of the *Parangon* of Tavernier (C1) were supplied by letters of Granjon's *St Augustin*, a much smaller face (266, 268). In the seventeenth century a number of books were printed at Antwerp in a mixture of Granjon's and Van Wolsschaten's (E2) Civilité types for the *St Augustin* body.

A2a. *A Variant used by Silvius* (fig. 22)

In some books printed by Willem Silvius at Antwerp in 1563–67 (67, 68, 80, 81, 90, 95, 103, 133)[1] the type is a mixture of Granjon's *Cicéro* and *St Augustin* Civilité faces with peculiar forms for some of the letters. The sorts peculiar to this fount are A E K c d e r; of the other capitals L O Q are from the *St Augustin* and the remainder from the *Cicéro*, and the P of both faces occurs: the lower-case letters all belong to the larger face, apart from the four sorts which only Silvius had. Silvius, as we remarked earlier,[2] was a scribe as well as a printer, and no doubt he had views of his own on type for the cursive. That would account for his special sorts; but he apparently had them grafted on Granjon's *St Augustin* in an imperfect state, before the capitals were ready.

Successive editions of the writing manual published by Silvius witness to a decline in the use of the variant fount. The earliest, in Dutch with the title *Eenen nieuwen A B C*, is dated 1564, and is set wholly in this fount (80); the edition of 1567, in French (103), has only a little of it at the end; that of 1568 (118) is set entirely in the *Cicéro* without special sorts.[3]

A3. *The 'Pré-Courante'* (figs. 23, 24)

A distinct type for lower-case letters in the Gothic script convention is used for headings in some books printed by Willem Silvius in the years 1565–76 (87, 104, 117, 133, 143, 144). It is evidently designed as a bold, ceremonious, and set *lettre françoise* to serve for headings and exordia in matter composed in type for the cursive hand. It imitates writing rather less slow and formal than *bâtarde*—something between

[1] See L. Willems, 'Ameet Tavernier en de Invoering van de Civilité-letter in Zuid-Nederland', *Tijdschrift voor Boek- en Bibliotheekwezen*, 5 (1907), pp. 241–63, where examples are reproduced.

[2] See above, p. 34.

[3] There is a copy of yet another edition, dated 1565, in the Newberry Library, Chicago: C. Clair, 'Willem Silvius', *The Library*, 5th ser., 14 (1959), at pp. 195–6. This we have not seen.

Introduction
de philosophie divine
de Viues,

Pour paruenir à la vraye cognoissance de
sapience chrestienne :

Traduite en François par M.
Guillaume Paradin :

Et de nouueau reueuë et corrigee en plusieurs
endroictz outre la derniere impression.

Auec vn tresample Indice des matieres
principales.

EX ÆQVITATE, ET

PRVDENTIA HONOS.

En Anuers,
Pour Robert Granjon.

Mil D^c. Lxv.

FIG. 23. J. L. Vives, *Introduction de philosophie divine*, translated by
G. Paradin, Antwerp, [W. Silvius] for R. Granjon, 1565. Title-page.
Types A1 + A2, A3. The lower-case letters in the first, fourth, and fifth
lines are the 'Pré-Courante' (see p. 48).

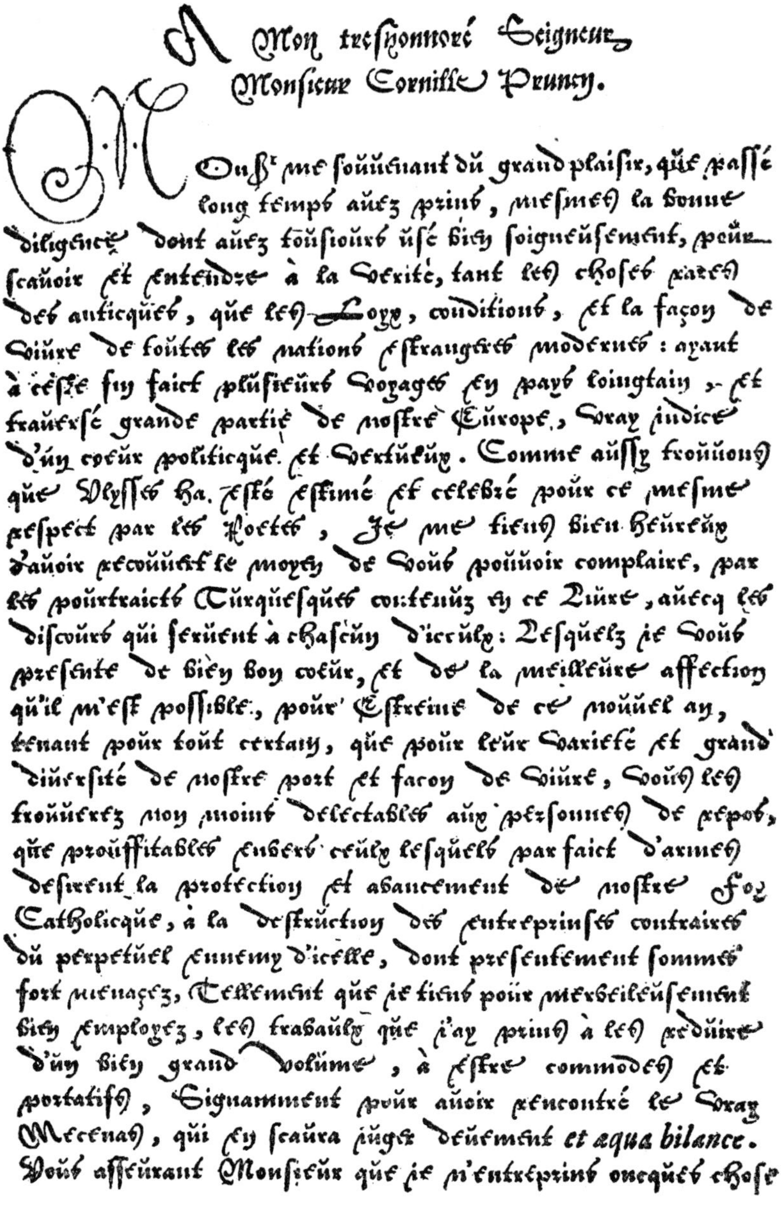

A Mon treshonnoré Seigneur
Monsieur Cornille Prunçy.

Nous me souuenant du grand plaisir, que passé long temps auez prins, mesmes la bonne diligence dont auez toussiours usé bien soigneusement, pour sçauoir et entendre à la Verité, tant les choses parts des anticques, que les Loyx, conditions, et la façon de viure de toutes les nations estrangéres modernes : ayant à ceste fin faict plusieurs Voyages en pays loingtain, et trauersé grande partie de nostre Europe, vray iudice d'un coeur politicque et Vertueux. Comme aussy trouuons que Vlysse ha esté estimé et célébré pour ce mesme respect par les Poetes, Je me tiens bien Heureux d'auoir recouuert le moyen de Vous pouuoir complaire, par les pourtraicts Turquesques contenuz en ce Liure, auecq les discours qui seruent à chascun d'iceulx : Lesquelz je Vous présente de bien bon coeur, et de la meilleure affection qu'il m'est possible, pour Estreine de ce nouuel an, tenant pour tout certain, que pour leur Varieté et grand diuersité de nostre port et façon de Viure, Vous les trouuerez moy moins délectables auy personnes de repos, que prouffitables enuers ceulx lesquelz par faict d'armes desirent la protection et abancement de nostre Foy Catholicque, à la destructioy des entreprinses contraires du perpétuel ennemy d'icelle, dont présentement sommes fort menacez, Tellement que je tiens pour merueileusement bien employez, les trabaulx que j'ay prins à les préduire d'un bien grand volume, à estre commodes et portatifs, Signamment pour auoir rencontré le Vray Mecenas, qui en sçaura juger deuement et aqua bilance. Vous asseurant Monsieur que je n'entreprins oncques chose

Fig. 24. A page of Nicolas de Nicolay, *Les Navigations, peregrinations et voyages*, Antwerp, W. Silvius, 1576. Types A3, A4. The heading is in the 'Pré-Courante', the text in the 'Dutch' *St Augustin*.

that and the *commune courante*. Granjon made a complete type in the same style a year or so later (A5, below), and Plantin named it 'Courante'. The lower case made for Silvius is so like it that there can be no doubt that it also was made by Granjon or that it was an experiment leading to the Courante.

A4. *The Dutch St Augustin* (figs. 24, 25)

We attribute this to Granjon tentatively on grounds of probability and style. Unlike the second of Granjon's script types (A2, above),

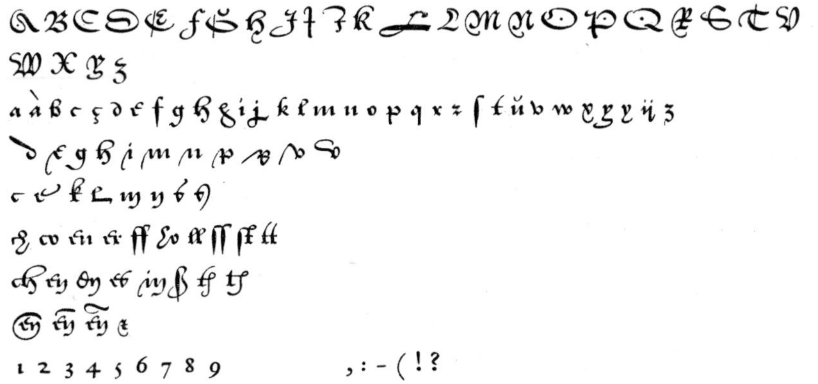

FIG. 25. The characters of the 'Dutch' *St Augustin* Civilité of Granjon cast in matrices belonging to Messrs. Johannes Enschedé en Zonen. Type A4.

this fits the true body of *St Augustin* or English. It is an extremely well-made type with the characteristic neatness and fluency of Granjon's scripts, but rendering a handwriting that in certain letters, e h t v, is Flemish rather than French, and it has abbreviations and ligatures fit only for that language. The u with a flick of the pen over it is not French either. It is a face peculiar to Willem Silvius as long as he lived, and almost as soon as he had begun to use it, in 1566 (94), he ceased to use any other Civilité. Thirteen of his books in our list have matter set in it. After the sale of printing material by Carel Silvius of Leyden in 1582,[1] the type is found in the work of Dutch printers at Leyden (247, 248, 250, 267, 292, 293) and Amsterdam (256, 263). It appears, therefore, to be a face cut for Silvius, and his close association with Granjon at the time of its cutting makes it likely that Granjon was the

[1] Enschedé, *Fonderies*, p. 53.

cutter. Although this type has all the usual sorts, Silvius mixed some of Granjon's other *St Augustin* (A2) with it, either by accident or for the sake of variety.

A set of the matrices belongs to Messrs. Enschedé (their No. 12). It has 106 sorts, including numerals: 27 capitals, 51 single lower-case letters, and 22 ligatures and compendia—a singularly well-preserved set. The provenance is from the typefoundry of Van der Putte at Amsterdam early in the eighteenth century.[1]

A5. *The Courante* (figs. 26, 27)

In January 1567 Plantin paid Granjon for punches and matrices for a *grosse françoise*,[2] and in the same year he showed a new face answering to that description in his *Index sive specimen characterum Christophori Plantini* (sign. D3, 'Pro Flacco'). In an unpublished specimen of his types printed about 1580[3] the same face is headed 'Courante sur le vray Texte' (i.e. for Great Primer). The punches and a set of matrices are at the Museum Plantin-Moretus. The sorts are very many: 156 punches and 180 matrices making 33 capitals, 65 single lower-case letters, and 41 ligatures, besides numerals and punctuation. No other type of the kind has so many alternative forms for the letters. The design has been described above (see under A3): a hybrid of *bâtarde* and cursive. The name 'Courante' does not fit it well, for it is decidedly a set hand. To us it looks cramped and spiritless in a too-late Gothic manner.

Plantin used his fount for books and jobs from 1567 onwards (102), and he took it to Leyden, where Raphelengius (in Plantin's name) also printed with it after him (235). One of that family must have parted with the original matrices to a local typefounder, for founts were owned by other printers in Holland (292, 306, 330), and a new set of matrices seems to have been made for the Moretus family in the seventeenth century.[4]

A set of matrices, perhaps originally Granjon's, is traceable at Lyons. Jean de Tournes had some of the type in 1583 (217), and two centuries later it was offered by the typefounder Delacolonge cast on English body as 'Civilité de Saint-Augustin' (518). By 1773 the e and perhaps one or two other sorts had broken and had been recut.

---

[1] Enschedé, *Fonderies*, p. 48.   [2] Early Inv., p. 38.

[3] Partly reproduced as an appendix to the paper of H. Carter on Plantin's types in *Gedenkboek der Plantin-dagen* (Antwerp, 1955) (= *De Gulden Passer*, 34 (1956), pp. 121–43), and in *The Library*, 5th Ser., 11 (1956), pp. 170–9.

[4] Early Inv., p. 118. The set existing in 1652 was justified, not for casting on *Texte*, but on the smaller body of *St Augustin*.

Men moet de herten met ootmoedicheyt ende
beleeftheyt winnen.

tuffche eerbaerheyt, beleefse ootmoedighe manieren,
Gy nu tue bequaem allen ionghen scholieren:
D'ootmoedicheyt (die alle eerbaeentheyt eeerstaet)
Canse met gheschickte krindtycheyt soo eexciexen,
Dat sy elck herte ghewinnen met suckey dat.
Daer sy is eiet dat zedicheyt te Bouen gaet.

r z ʒ ſ ſſ s ʒ 6 ʒ z tt ʒ

Hceeryck wordt hier alle consten onderhouwen   Duer glorie end' eer haer soeckter forckhurdich:
Eere can den traghen tot arbeyt houwen.   Maer eerloos sijn maeckt den menfche onuerdutsich.

C 2

FIG. 26. A page of [Peter Heyns], *ABC, of Exemplen*, Antwerp, C. Plantin, 1568. Types A5, A6, B3. The heading is in the Bastarde.

A6. *The Bastarde* (figs. 26, 27, 28)

Granjon sold to Plantin, probably in 1567,[1] the punches and matrices
for a lower case, which, mated with the capitals and punctuation of

FIG. 27. The characters of Granjon's Courante and Bastarde cast in matrices at the
Museum Plantin-Moretus. Types A5, A6.

the Courante (A5, above), made a distinct face representing the writing-
masters' *bâtarde* of the time. Plantin's folio specimen of about 1580
shows it as 'Bastarde' on the body of *Texte*. The bowls of the letters
are big in relation to the ascenders and descenders, so that this was a
useful bold face for the headings to matter set in smaller script types

[1] Early Inv., pp. 38, 47.

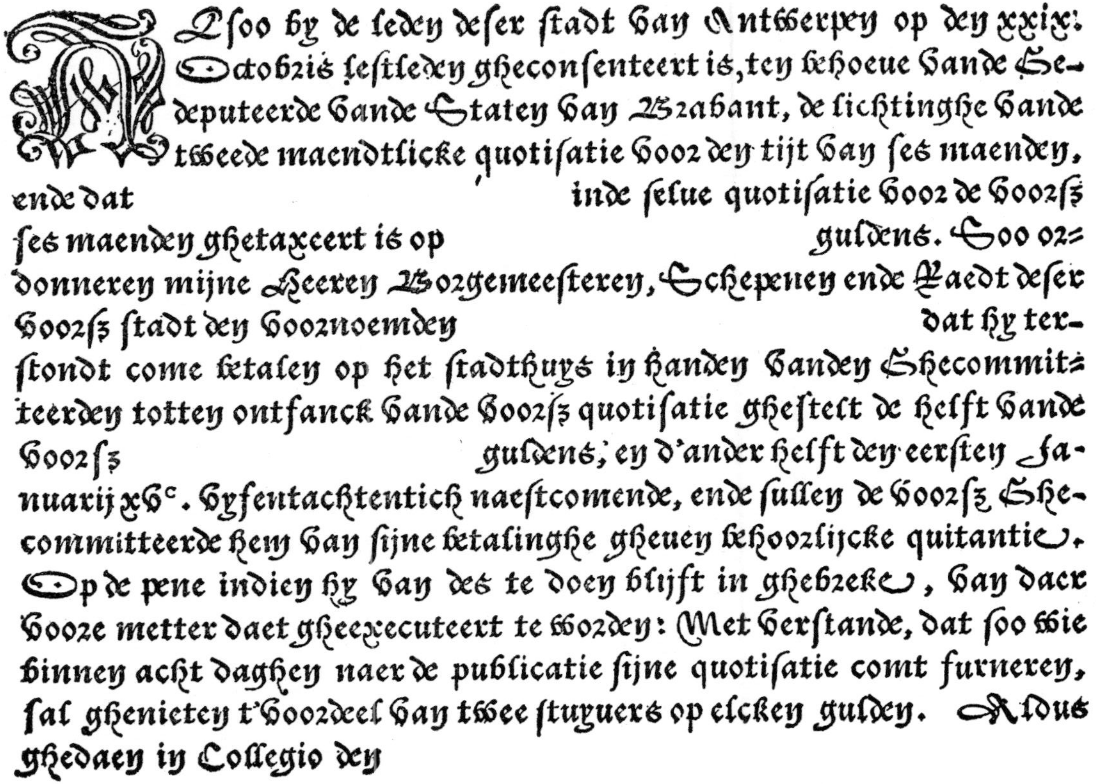
Alsoo by de leden deser stadt van Antwerpen op den xxix.
Octobris lestleden gheconsenteert is, ten behoeue vande Ge-
deputeerde vande Staten van Brabant, de lichtinghe vande
tweede maendtlicke quotisatie voor den tijt van ses maenden,
ende dat inde selue quotisatie voor de voorsz
ses maenden ghetaxeert is op guldens. Soo or-
donneren mijne Heeren Borghemeesteren, Schepenen ende Raedt deser
voorsz stadt den voornoemden dat hy ter-
stondt come betalen op het stadthuys in handen vanden Ghecommit-
teerden totten ontfanck vande voorsz quotisatie ghestelt de helft vande
voorsz guldens, en d'ander helft den eersten Ja-
nuarij xvc. vyfentachtentich naestcomende, ende sullen de voorsz Ghe-
committeerde hem van sijne betalinghe gheuen behoorlijcke quitantie.
Op de pene indien hy van des te doen blijft in ghebreke, van daer
voore metter daet gheexecuteert te worden: Met verstande, dat soo wie
binnen acht daghen naer de publicatie sijne quotisatie comt furneren,
sal ghenieten t'voordeel van twee stuyvers op elcken gulden. Aldus
ghedaen in Collegio den

FIG. 28. A form of demand for the payment of tax to the City of Antwerp printed by Plantin *c.* 1584. Type A6 (Granjon's Bastarde).

and, on its own, for jobbing. The taste is pronouncedly Gothic, the curves being stressed and kinked in the *fractura* manner.

Plantin printed with the Bastarde first in 1568 (112–16), and often thereafter for controversial pamphlets, edicts, and forms. He took it to Leyden (227), where it was used later by Raphelengius (249). Like the Courante (292), it found its way to the press of the town clerk, Jan van Hout, at Leyden (215). It was fairly widespread in Holland from 1612 until 1649, when it vanishes from there.

The punches at the Museum Plantin-Moretus are for 34 single letters and 14 ligatures.[1] The set of 60 matrices is for these and 11 accented letters.

The Bastarde appears in the printing of Jean de Tournes II at Lyons in 1578 (165). Delacolonge of Lyons showed it in his specimen-book in 1773, headed 'Civilité de Gros-romain'.

This face is easily confused with a copy of it made in Holland in the seventeenth century (H9, below, p. 85).

Woodcut letters very closely resembling those of the Courante and the Bastarde are to be seen in the writing-manual of Jean de Beauchesne and John Baildon published in London in 1570.[2] The correspondence is too close to be accidental; but it seems impossible to tell whether De Beauchesne, who came to England about 1565,[3] copied the types or provided models for them.

A7. *Plantin's unfinished Françoise sur la Garramonde* (fig. 29)

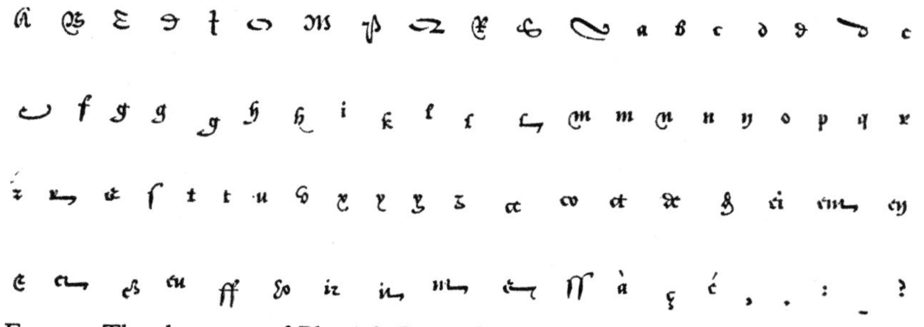

FIG. 29. The characters of Plantin's Lettre françoise for the body of Garamonde cut by Granjon *c.* 1566, cast in matrices at the Museum Plantin-Moretus. Type A7.

On 7 December 1566 Granjon signed a contract with Plantin agreeing to sell him the punches and matrices for 'la petite francoyse quil

---

[1] Early Inv., p. 38.

[2] *A Booke containing divers sortes of hands*, S.T.C. 6446. The copy in the British Museum is dated 1571, but one of the previous year was known to R. Dickson and J. P. Edmond, *Annals of Scottish Printing* (Cambridge, 1890), p. 378.

[3] E. J. Worman, *Alien Members of the Book-Trade during the Tudor Period* (1906), p. 2.

a faict dernierement en ceste ville'.[1] Plantin entered them in his inventory of 1572 as 'Garramonde Lectre françoise de Granjon point achevee'.[2] The lower case is complete, save for some doublets, but there are only eleven capitals. It is curious that matrices were made from an incomplete set of punches. It is a wonderfully delicate miniature letter. The punches and matrices are preserved at the Museum Plantin-Moretus.

A8. *The Civilité de Petit Romain of De Tournes* (fig. 30)

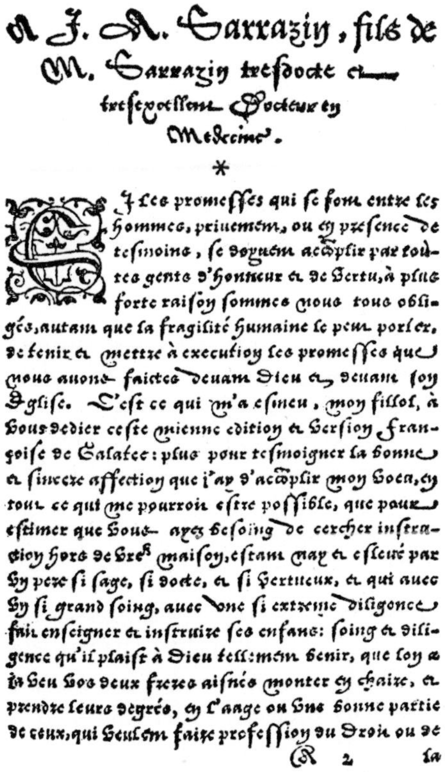
A I. A. Sarrazin, fils de
M. Sarrazin tresdocte et
tresexcellent Docteur en
Medecine.
*
Si les promesses qui se font entre les hommes, priuement, ou en presence de tesmoins, se doyuent accomplir par toutes gens d'honneur et de vertu, à plus forte raison sommes nous tous obligés, autant que la fragilité humaine le peut porter, de tenir et mettre à execution les promesses que nous auons faictes deuant Dieu et deuant son Eglise. C'est ce qui m'a esmeu, mon fillol, à vous dedier ceste mienne edition et version Françoise de Galatee: plus pour tesmoigner la bonne et sincere affection que i'ay d'accomplir mon voeu, en tout ce qui me pourroit estre possible, que pour estimer que vous ayez besoing de chercher instruction hors de vre maison, estant nay et esleué par vn pere si sage, si docte, et si vertueux, et qui auec vn si grand soing, auec vne si extreme diligence fait enseigner et instruire ses enfans: soing et diligence qu'il plaist à Dieu tellement benir, que lon a ia veu vos deux freres aisnés monter en chaire, et prendre leurs degrés, en l'aage ou vne bonne partie de ceux, qui veulent faire profession du Droit ou de
A 2 la

FIG. 30. The opening page of the foreword to I. de La Case, *Le Galatée*, [Geneva], J. de Tournes, 1598. Type A8, a lettre françoise for Garamond (Long Primer) body differing from A7.

A book (246) printed in 1587 by Jean de Tournes II at Geneva is the earliest of which we know to show a Civilité type on the same body as Plantin's 'petite francoyse' (A7, above), that is to say *Petit Romain* or Long Primer. The two faces, though much alike, are quite distinct.

[1] Early Inv., pp. 38, 43. [2] Ibid., p. 33.

The likeness and the fact that all the other script types of De Tournes are by Granjon are grounds enough for attributing this one to him. It is shown in the specimen-book of Delacolonge at Lyons, 1773 (518), as 'Civilité de Petit-romain'.

B. GOTHIC SCRIPT TYPES BY PHILIPPE DANFRIE

B1 and B2. *The St Augustin of Danfrie and Breton and the Gros Romain of Breton* (figs. 9, 11, 16, 31, 32)

The type in which these partners set their books was cast on a large body of *St Augustin* for which it was rather too big, so that the long letters in adjoining lines overlap one another. As punchcutting it is little inferior to the only earlier face of the same kind, Granjon's *Cicéro*. The letters, however, are cast with wider intervals between them, so that lines set in them appear rather less solid and coherent than those in Granjon's books. The design of the lower case is virtually the same in both, but the capitals differ a good deal, and Danfrie's are more intricate and fantastic.

Breton went on using this type after the lapse of Danfrie's name from the imprints in 1559 until the year of his death, 1571. A book was printed in it by Breton's widow in the following year. An inventory of the goods of the deceased Breton made on 2 May 1571[1] discloses the following:

Item les poinçons et matrices dune lettre françoise du corps de saint augustin garni de ses moulles. . . . Item les poinçons et matrices dune lettre françoise du corps de gros romain. . . .

The smaller face may be assumed to have been the one used for texts by Danfrie and Breton, for it is easy to believe that Danfrie, the punchcutter, made the type to Breton's order or ceded his rights in it to Breton. The second item, the similar face for Great Primer body, cannot be identified with certainty, for we do not know that a type of that description is to be seen in Breton's printing. However, some fifteen years after Breton's death a Civilité type on *Gros Romain* body was used with Danfrie's *St. Augustin* in two books printed by Claude Micard in Paris (238, 281). From then onwards the two types are found in association. Probably the larger was the *Gros Romain* in the inventory of Breton's goods.

The punches for the smaller type passed to Guillaume Le Bé II. In his inventory made about 1598 he put 114 punches (but no matrices)

[1] Paris, Archives nat., Minutier central, Étude cxxii, liasse 129, fol. 10.

for 'Lettres francoises de St Augustin danfrie'.[1] Le Bé must at one time have had matrices as well, for he sent a specimen of this with

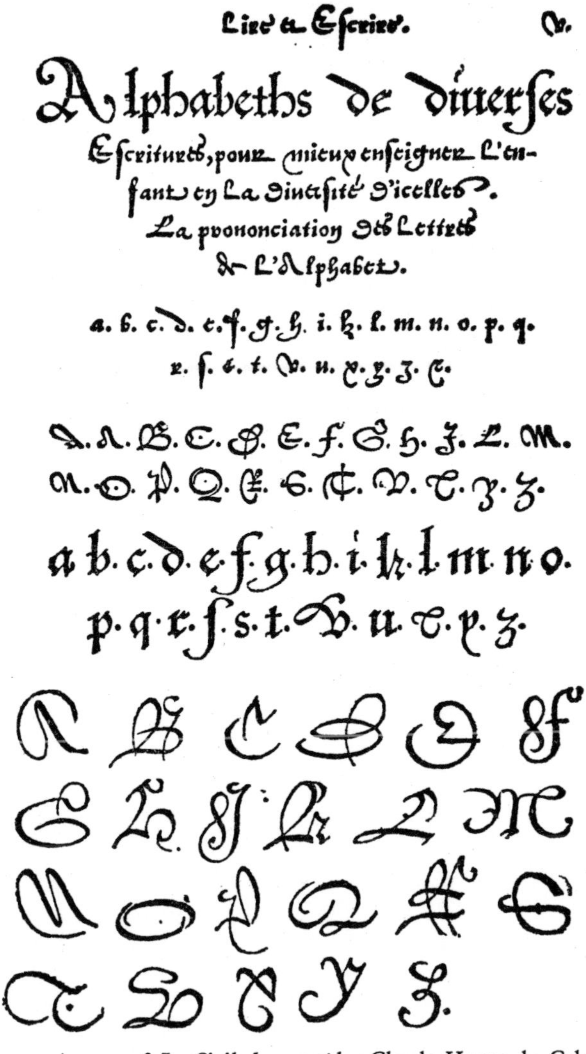

FIG. 31. A page of *La Civile honesteté* by Claude Hours de Calviac, Paris, R. Breton. 1560, showing the alphabets of Civilité fashion regularly used by Breton. Type B1.

others of his types to Jean Moretus about 1599, and this specimen is still kept in the Plantin-Moretus archives.[2] We know of no occurrence of the face in print between the years 1599 and 1742. In the latter year

[1] S. Morison, *Inventaire de la fonderie Le Bé*, p. 21.
[2] MPM, Arch.. vol. 153, fol. 20g.

Advertissement au lecteur.

Ce afin que pas ony ci'euſt excuſe
De ſoucte Dieu, Marot auec ſa muſe
Chanta iadis iuſques au tiers des antiques,
En grand David, qui ſont hebraiques,

Sa harpe fit parler premierement,
Et puis ſouſit ſa plume & element,
Ceſte fuy que du peuple françois
Dieu fuſt loué & cnême & de croix.

Petite quatraine adiouſtez ſur les Ꝑ.
choſe ꝑ faiſons & l'an, & l'année, ꝑui
Pſalme 147. a Dieu.

L'eſture qui comme mont de plaine,
De neige auſſi blanche que laine,
Et qui ꝟient la bonne eſpandez,
Sont auſſi ꝑment comme cendre.

Febureie, du pſalme 65.
L'eau qui ꝟes ruiſſeaux degorge,
Dieu la terre nourrit:
A fin que le froment ꝟ rouge,
Puiſſe croiſtre & mourir.

Mars, du pſalme 65.
La ſaiſon ꝟonnée & ceints,

FIG. 32. Two pages from P. Du Val, *Psalme par quatrains de la puissance, sapience, & bonté de Dieu*, Paris, C. Micard, [1585?]. Types B1, B2.

the 'Civilité de St. Augustin' begins a second career in the *Épreuves générales des caractères* of Claude Lamesle, typefounder in Paris.[1] Here it is shown (on fol. 38) with fatter forms for f and long s and their doublets than those cut by Danfrie and with the addition of a fatter initial v and capital L, while a ligature of lz is pressed into service for capital K, previously not represented in the fount.

In this renovated state the *St Augustin* was included in the *Épreuves des caractères* of Jacques François Rosart, punchcutter and typefounder, issued at Brussels in 1768, with a footnote: 'Gravé par feu le Sr. Grand-jant à Paris'. It is hard to tell what construction to put on this note by Rosart: perhaps he thought that Granjon, who cut other Civilité types, must have cut this; perhaps he knew that Philippe Grandjean (who died in 1714)[2] had remodelled it. The new letters look as though the typefounder who owned the punches wanted the face to be brought up to date in fashion and made more like the *Gros Romain*.

We believe that all subsequent examples of printing in this type show it in the revised state. The punches, preserved by Messrs. Deberny-Peignot in Paris (fig. 16), are divisible into survivors of the original set cut by Danfrie and others of more recent date and by different hands.[3]

The larger of these two scripts differs a good deal from the smaller in the shapes given to the letters—to the capitals particularly—and it is not nearly such an attractive face. It, also, appears in the *Épreuves* of Lamesle in 1742 (fol. 47), where it is named 'Civilité au Corps de Gros Romain, Numero XLIX'.[4] Lamesle, according to Fournier le Jeune, succeeded Pierre Cot in a typefounding business begun about 1670,[5] and his specimens of 1742 are clearly the work of several hands over a long span of time. The bigger Civilité may very easily have been the one for which Guillaume Le Bé II owned the punches, entered in his inventory about 1598 as 'Lettre francoise gros rom. C' following those for Danfrie's *St Augustin*.

This does not mean that Danfrie cut the *Gros Romain*. Breton may have got another artist to make him a larger face matching the one by Danfrie. The larger, the Great Primer, looks like the work of a skilful man who was less of an artist than Danfrie. Moreover the letter 'C'

[1] No. 459 in our Appendix. The sheets were reissued in 1760 as the *Épreuves des caractères* of Lamesle's successors, Gando père et fils.

[2] F. A. Duprat, *Historie de l'Imprimerie Impériale de France* (Paris, 1861), p. 87.

[3] We have to acknowledge the kindness of Messrs. Deberny-Peignot in answering our inquiries and supplying us with a proof and a photograph of this material.

[4] Reproduced in D. B. Updike, *Printing Types*, 3rd ed. (1962), fig. 143.

[5] *Manuel typographique*, ii (Paris, 1766), p. xxv.

at the end of the entry made by Le Bé cannot have stood for Danfrie: it is probably short for 'céans', meaning that the punches were made on his premises. It seems not unlikely that it was a face left by Danfrie in an unfinished state and furnished much later with the sorts needed to complete it.

B3. *The 'Petite Augustine Invention de Hamon'* (figs. 15, 26, 33, 34)

There is little more than inference to support the attribution of this face to Danfrie as punchcutter.[1] His name occurs with those of Jean

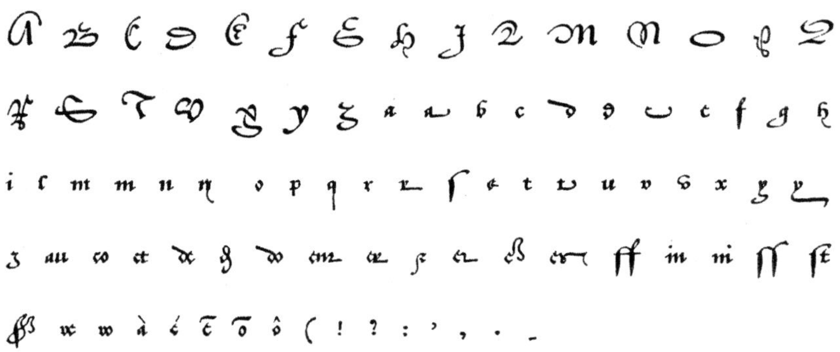

FIG. 33. The characters of Plantin's Petite Augustine françoise cast in matrices at the Museum Plantin-Moretus. Type B3.

Le Royer and Pierre Hamon in the imprint of a translation by Claude Pontoux, *Harangue de Sainct Basile le grand a ses ieunes disciples et neveux* dated at Paris in 1561 (52). This book is probably the first in which the type was used, though one other, Hamon's writing-manual, of the same year has a sonnet set in it at the beginning (51).

The name 'Invention de Hamon' was given to the type by Plantin in his accounts for 1564.[2] The same word was used by Hamon himself in the title of his book, *L'Alphabet de linuention des lettres en diverses escritures*, and it clearly means that Hamon was what we should call the 'designer' of the type. Of the other two partners in the imprint, Le Royer was a printer: the inference that Danfrie made the type is a strong one.

Plantin acquired the punches with a set of matrices and a mould soon after his return to Antwerp from Paris in 1563.[3] He is the only printer

---

[1] The punches for this face, preserved at the Museum Plantin-Moretus, and the oldest of those belonging to Messrs. Deberny-Peignot for Breton's *St Augustin* (B1) are alike in shape and style of workmanship: cf. our figs. 15, 16.

[2] Early Inv., p. 27. [3] Ibid.

DE L'ŒUVRE DE HAMON
SONNET

A MONSEIGNEUR
LE ANRE

DVC D'ORLEANS.

Qui voudra voir les forces de nature,
Et contemplez ses present les plus beaux,
M'admire point ses divers animaux
Qui sont pourtraitz d'vne estrange peinture,
M'admire point ses fruitz ny sa verdure
My ses couleurs des plumes des oyseaux:
Mais bien sa main & ses beaux traictz nouueaux
D'vne si rare et si belle escoiture,
En sous Monsieur, heureux vous pouuez estre
Que c'est espvit vous appelle son maistre,
Et plus heureux qu'il soit ne de ce tempz.
Car ses beaux traictz de sa plume naifue
En cent facons passent sa couleur viue
Et des oyseaux et des fleurs du printempz.

P. Ronsard.

Fig. 34. Sonnet by Ronsard prefacing Pierre Hamon's *Alphabet de linuention des lettres en diverses escritures*, Paris, J. Le Royer, 1561. Type B3.

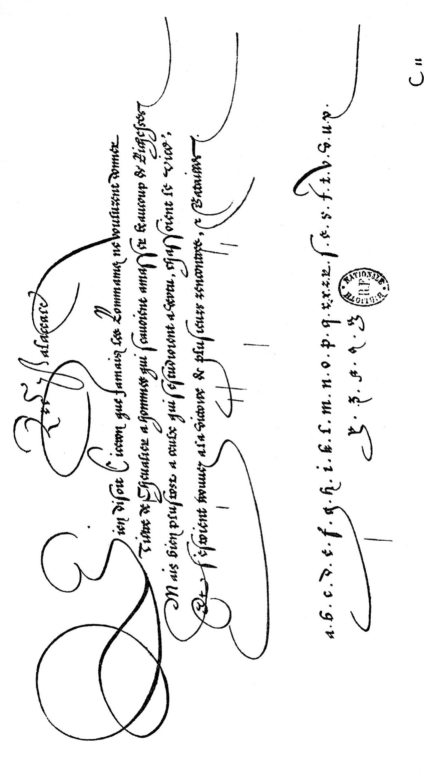

Fig. 35. A model for Lettre Palaceale in Pierre Hamon's *Alphabet de plusieurs sortes de lettres*, Paris, R. Estienne, 1566. This style of writing appears to have been the pattern for the type named 'Petite Augustine inuention de Hamon' (our B3, shown in figs. 33, 34).

in whose work the face occurs after 1561. He did not, so far as we know, ascribe it to any punchcutter; but two of his inventories, those of his founts in 1575 and of his typefounding equipment in 1581, which he did not write himself, describe it as cut by Pierre Haultin. Haultin's name would have been familiar to the compilers of these documents, while Hamon's was not, and we suppose the attribution was a mistake.[1]

The fashion of the letters is not that of the ordinary cursive handwriting of the time but an elaborate and artificial masterpiece worthy of such an accomplished scribe. Its similarity to a model by him for a *lettre palaceale*[2] suggests a connexion with the business of the royal household. The 87 punches surviving at the Museum Plantin-Moretus are beautifully cut. The 88 matrices provide 22 capitals (O is missing), 33 single lower-case letters, 20 ligatures, and 5 accented sorts.

B4, 5. *The Types of the Graphometre* (fig. 36)

Many years after his other ventures in publishing, Danfrie wrote and printed his *Déclaration de l'usage du graphometre* in 1597. The subject is an instrument that he had invented for measuring angles. It is set in a pair of script types on a body of *Gros Parangon* or Double Pica, a *bâtarde* for the headings, and a more cursive type for the text. The capitals are common to both. The *lettre françoise* represented by the text-type is a later development than the one imitated by the types of 1557–61. The shading is rounded, not angular, and the shapes are generally simpler. The capitals, particularly, have lost their Gothic intricacies.

The presumption that Danfrie would have cut the types seen first in a book that he wrote and printed is confirmed by an item in the inventory of Guillaume Le Bé made about 1620: 'Lettre françoise de Parengon danfrie 174 m[atrices]'.[3] The number of matrices is enough to take in both the types of the *Graphometre* and there can be little doubt that the entry relates to them.

In 1598 Danfrie resigned his appointment as 'Graveur général des effigies des monnaies de France' in favour of his son of the same names.[4]

---

[1] Other types by Haultin which Plantin owned are found in the printing done by Haultin himself and his nephew, Jérôme; but this is not.

[2] In *Alphabet de plusieurs sortes de lettres par Pierre Hamon* (1566), our Fig. 35.

[3] S. Morison, *L'Inventaire de la fonderie Le Bé* (Paris, 1957), p. 21.

[4] F. Mazerolle, *Les Médailleurs français du XVᵉ siècle au milieu du XVIIᵉ siècle*, i (Paris, 1902), p. lxxxi.

La maniere de faire cartes Geographiques

de telle grandeur et estendue de paic, que Voudra le Geographe.

Chapitre Xj.

Apres auoir enseigné à prendre les longueurs
et semblablement les trauerses de plusieurs choses
notables cy deuant mises en dessein, et que Vous
ayez Volonté de faire la description de toute sa Pro-
uince, Vous le pouuez faire par la pratique cy deuant
enseignee. Posez le cas que la figure cy deuant soit
le commencement de la description que Voulez faire:
Vous auez icy à considerer de quel costé Vous Voulez
augmenter ledit dessein, car pour toute la description
que Vous ferez, Vous n'estes subjet tant que ceste o-
peration soit finie de plus compter nulle espace d'V-
ne station à l'autre, d'autant que Vous auez toutes
les mesures et espace des choses notables cottees
à ladite figure: partant Vous pouuez poser l'Obser-
uateur dessus quel poinct cotté à la figure que Vou-
drez: posez le donc dessus l'Vn des poincts qui Vous
puisse seruir de premiere station , comme seroit E,

FIG. 36. Philippe Danfrie, *Declaration de l'usage du graphometre*, Paris, P. Danfrie, 1597. Types B4, B5.

The later history of these types and the material for casting them is unknown, except that a book was printed in them in 1626 (363).

C. GOTHIC SCRIPT TYPES BY AMEET TAVERNIER
C1, C2. *The Parangon and Mediane Geschreven* (figs. 12, 37, 38)

A rhetorician of Ghent, Marcus van Vaernewyck, left an account in verse of the making of types after the fashion of handwriting by Ameet Tavernier at Antwerp in the year 1558.[1] In a number of the books that he printed Tavernier used two of such types. Besides cutting punches and printing books, Tavernier cast type for sale, and his script types were used by other printers in the Netherlands during and after his lifetime, which ended in 1570.[2]

The two types have been described as a *Parangon* (Paragon) and a *Médiane* (Pica),[3] those being the bodies on which Tavernier cast them, though the face of the larger type was too big for a Paragon body. The first book in which either can be found is a Flemish version of Erasmus on manners for children, *Goede manierliicke Seden* (17), dated 1559 with the imprint of Jan van Waesberghe at Antwerp. This is set in the bigger face. The smaller occurs with it in a book of the following year published, also at Antwerp, by Jean Bellere (37) and in others bearing Tavernier's own imprint from 1561 onwards.[4]

The style of these *geschreven letters* by Tavernier is markedly different from those of the French script types that we have been considering. There are archaic forms for some letters, and the general effect is more rugged and has a touch of humour about it. Evidently Tavernier was basing himself on a handwriting still medieval, and a scrivener's rather than a writing-master's accomplishment. Its Flemish character confined it to the Low Countries, whereas the French Civilité types were found acceptable outside the country of origin.

The smaller of Tavernier's scripts was obtainable in Antwerp as late as 1650 (384), and the larger could be had in 1612 (332), while founts, containing many letters of Tavernier's larger type (E2a) were in use as late as 1834 (617).[5] By some means, a set, now defective, of

---

[1] *Den Spieghel der Nederlandscher audtheyt* (Ghent, 1568), Book IV, fol. 141, reprinted by Sabbe and Audin, *Die Civilité-Schriften*, as fig. 14.

[2] M. Parker, K. Melis, H. D. L. Vervliet, 'Typographica Plantiniana III. Ameet Tavernier, Punchcutter (ca. 1522–1570), *De Gulden Passer*, 39 (1961), pp. 17–76.

[3] Ibid., p. 59.

[4] For the books printed by Tavernier, see M. Sabbe, 'Bijdrage tot de Bibliographie van Ameet Tavernier', *De Gulden Passer*, 7 (1929), pp. 168–201; H. D. L. Vervliet, 'Rectifications et additions à la bibliographie d'Aimé Tavernier, imprimeur et tailleur de caractères anversois', in *Gutenberg Jahrbuch*, 36 (Mainz, 1961), pp. 122–8.

[5] See under E2a, following.

Den wtersten wille van

LOVVYS PORQVIN

Seur Hem ghecomponeert in prose by maniere van een Lieflijck Testament, Inhoudende veel schoone Leeringhen, tot Instructie ende stichtinghe van zijnen Kinderen. Oock seer nut, oorboor en prouffakelijck allen ouders, om haren kinderen hier med tonderwijsen, om daer door te comen (met GODS hulpe) tot een goet eerlijck leuen, ende een salich steruen.

Ende tot meerder affectie vanden Jonghen Leser, heeft tselfde by eenen Anthonius Verensis uter prose In Rhetorijcke doen stellen. Het werck Lowys voornoemt, wt liefden zijne lieue ende beminde kinderen tot een memoriael in zijnder ghedenckenisse heeft achtergelaten.

ESAIAS XXXVIII.

Beschickt v huys Wilt Godt aenrueen,
Want ghy sult steruen en niet Leuen.

Gheprint TAntwerpen, inde gulden Hoose by, Ameet Tauernier Lettersther, An. 1563.

FIG. 37. The title-page of *Den wtersten Wille van Lowys Porquin*, Antwerp, A. Tavernier, 1563. Types C1, C2.

matrices for the *Parangonne* found its way into the collection in Plantin's house, though none of the documents there throws light on its acquisition. The 87 matrices provide a complete lower case and some interesting ligatures and compendia—a precious link with medieval writing.[1] Only twelve of the matrices for capitals are left.

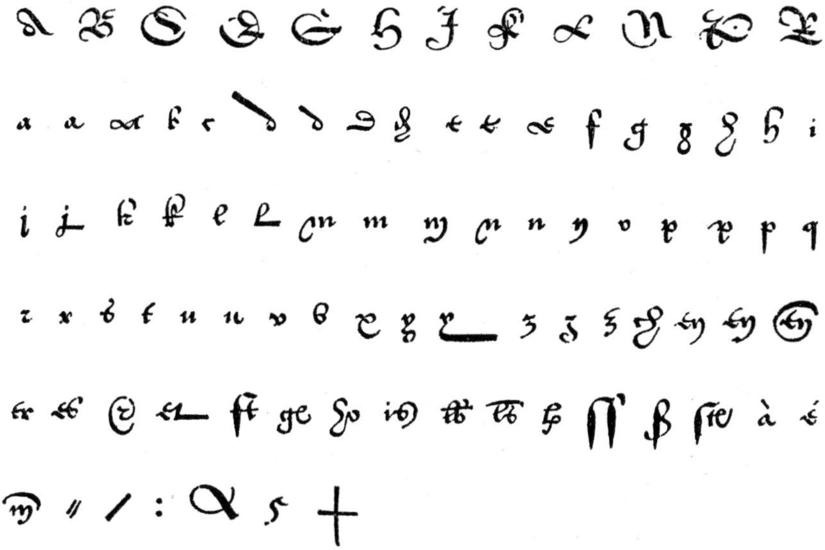

FIG. 38. The characters of the Paragon script type of Tavernier cast in matrices at the Museum Plantin-Moretus. Type C1.

Tavernier had a wealth of large initial letters of the Civilité fashion, some of them in the form of type. On 2-line Pica body he had an alphabet of capitals, now represented by matrices for eight letters at the Museum Plantin-Moretus.[2] He also made some very big Gothic initials in the intricate ornamental manner of engrossing, no doubt cut in wood but perhaps reduplicated by casting in sand moulds.

D. A GOTHIC SCRIPT TYPE BY HENDRIK VAN DEN KEERE

D1. *Van den Keere's Mediane Geschreven* (fig. 39)

This punchcutter, a Fleming otherwise called Henri Du Tour, belonged to the generation after Tavernier's. Evidence of his activity does not go much farther back than 1569. His typefoundry at Ghent had been the property of his father of the same names and probably

---

[1] The matrices are numbered MA 163.
[2] Included in MA 163.

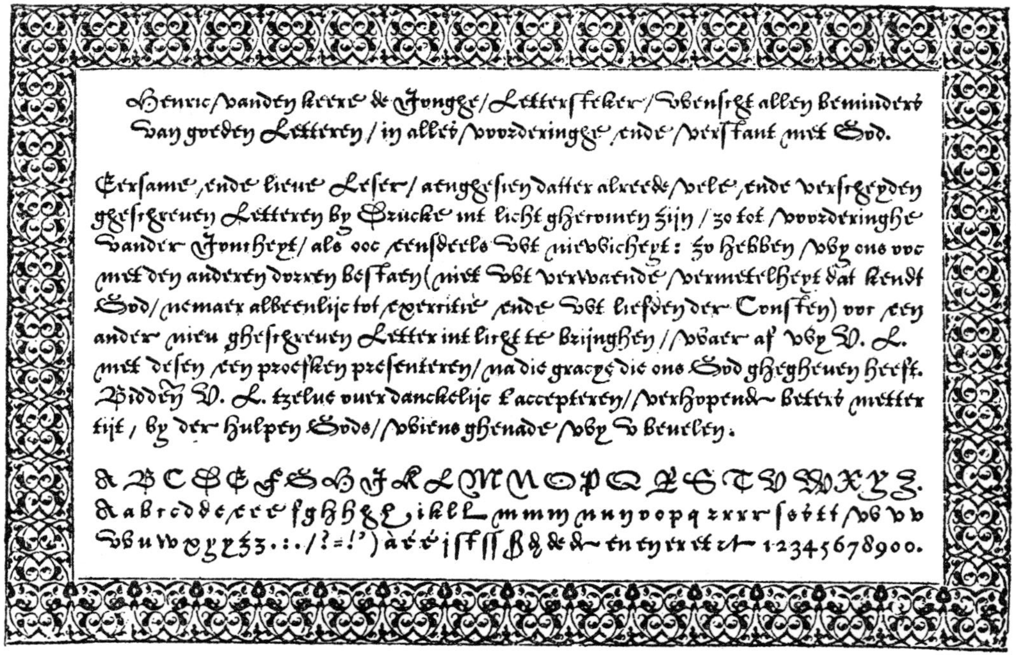

Henric vanden Keere de Jonghe/ Lettersteker/ wenscht allen beminders van goeden Letteren/ in alles voorderinghe/ ende verstant met God.

Eersame/ ende lieve Leser/ aenghesien datter alreede vele/ ende verscheyden ghesneden Letteren by Drucke int licht ghecomen zijn/ zo tot voorderinghe vander Jonkheyt/ als oock eensdeels wt nieusghierheyt: zo hebben wy ons oock met den anderen daeren bestaen (niet wt verwaende vermetelheyt dat kendt God/ maer alleenlijc tot exercitie/ ende wt liefden der Consten) om een ander nieu ghesneden Letter int licht te bringhen/ waer af wy U. L. met desen een proefken presenteren/ na die gracye die ons God ghegheven heeft. Bidden U. L. tzelve om danckelijc taccepteren/ verhopende beter metter tijt/ by der hulpen Gods/ wiens ghenade wy U bevelen.

A B C D E F G H J K L M N O P Q R S T V W X Y Z.

1234567890 0.

Fig. 39. A specimen advertising a script type by Hendrik van den Keere, *c.* 1570. Type D1.

succeeded one established in 1536 by Joos Lambrecht, since three types in the inventory of the younger Van den Keere were ascribed to Lambrecht.[1] From 1569 until his death in 1580 Van den Keere undertook the typefounding for Plantin's office and cut some thirty new typefaces for him.[2] The typefounder's widow sold all his material to Plantin in 1581, subject to a condition that her son or her husband's foreman might buy any of it back again.[3]

The Museum Plantin-Moretus has the only copies of a little specimen of Civilité type (125) with wording in Flemish to this effect:

Henric vanden keere the younger, letter-cutter, wishes divine furtherance and favour in all things to all lovers of good type.

Honoured and beloved reader, seeing that many and various script types made for the benefit of youth and partly for novelty have by now appeared in print we (not out of pride or presumption, God knows, but in the ordinary exercise of our art and for the love of it) have seen fit to produce another, and hereby, as God has given us grace, we lay before you a small specimen of it. We beg you to accept it, and meanwhile we hope to do better in time with God's help, and pray His blessing upon you.

In the inventory of the foundry drawn up in 1580[4] are entered the punches, numbering 120, and matrices for a 'Mediane gheschreven letter', and a list of the material subsequently claimed by the foreman, Thomas De Vechter, includes the matrices for the 'Mediane gheschreven letter van Mr. Henrick'.[5] The punches were evidently left with Plantin, and the set, now of 116, is still in his house.[6]

The type was used by a printer at Louvain in 1571 (129a) and in a book published at Antwerp in 1572, the *Epitres morales* of Tixier (130), where it serves for the Flemish version put beside the French. Jan van Hout bought a fount of it for his use in the Raedhuys at Leyden (215), probably soon after his press was set up there in 1577, and he named Van den Keere as the supplier.[7] De Vechter, once foreman to Van den Keere, settled in Leyden in 1584,[8] and he probably supplied the numerous Dutch and Belgian printers who made use of this face.

---

[1] Early Inv., pp. 80–82. For Van den Keere, see *Gedenkboek der Plantin-dagen 1555–1955* (Antwerp, 1956), pp. 261–2. [2] Early Inv., pp. 138–9.
[3] *Correspondance de Christophe Plantin*, vi (Antwerp and The Hague, 1916), pp. 238–9.
[4] Early Inv., pp. 53–66. [5] Ibid., p. 81. [6] No. ST47.
[7] W. I. C. Rammelman Elsevier, 'De voormalige Drukkerij op het Raadhuis der Stad Leiden, 1577–1610', in *Nieuwe Reeks van Werken van de Maatschappij der Nederlandsche Letterkunde te Leiden*, 10 (1857), pp. 282–5.
[8] H. F. Wijnman, 'Thomas De Vechter, Lettergieter te Leiden', *Het Boek*, 28 (1948), p. 150.

The matrices came into the possession of the Voskens family, type-founders at Amsterdam. The widow of Dirk Voskens (after 1689–90) showed this script in her specimen-sheet,[1] and about thirty years later it was displayed in a specimen by Anthonie and Hendrik Bruyn, also of Amsterdam (445). When, in 1847, Messrs Enschedé bought part of typefoundry of Elix & Co. of Amsterdam, they acquired these matrices with the rest of Bruyn's stock.[2] The set of 102 matrices is *Cicéro d'écriture*, No. 14 in the firm's inventory.

Van den Keere's is a beautiful version of the script, very skilfully cut and founded. It represents a hand not much different from the French, without the Flemish mannerism of Tavernier's.

E. THE GOTHIC SCRIPT TYPES OF VAN WOLSSCHATEN (fig. 40)

Three inferior Civilité types used at Antwerp during the seventeenth and eighteenth centuries are attributable to the typefoundry of Van Wolsschaten.

Of this family of typefounders very little is known; but the records of the Guild of St. Luke at Antwerp[3] and documents at the Museum Plantin-Moretus establish approximately a succession of masters of the foundry from Gheeraerd I van Wolsschaten in 1596 to Johannes Baptista in 1752. The Museum has six specimen-sheets[4] issued by this firm at various times, of which one, probably attributable to Melchior van Wolsschaten *c.* 1710, shows three Civilité faces of different sizes.

E1. *Van Wolsschaten's Paragon* (figs. 40, 41)

The biggest, headed 'Texte Gheschreven' in the specimen, is on a Paragon body and evidently a copy of Tavernier's type of that description (C1, above). It is easy to mistake one for the other, and the curlier terminals to the strokes of Van Wolsschaten's letters are the easiest means to telling them apart. An incomplete set of matrices for this Paragon survives at the Museum Plantin-Moretus,[5] though the records there do nothing to explain its presence. Of the capitals Y and Z are missing, and the lower case lacks about a dozen sorts. The earliest

---

[1] B.M., Harl. 5930, No. 541; Mus. Plantin-Moretus, Folia Varia II, fol. 105; Stichting Museum Enschedé, Haarlem, reproduced in *Type Specimen Facsimiles*, ed. John Dreyfus (London, 1963), No. 8. The last two collections also have an undated, but later, specimen of Clerk, Voskens & Co., which shows the type.

[2] Enschedé, *Fonderies*, pp. 51–56. See Early Inv., p. 65 (LMA25).

[3] Ph. Rombouts and Th. van Lerius, *De Liggeren der Antwerpsche Sint-Lucasgilde* (Antwerp, 1872).

[4] MPM, Arch., Fol. Var. II, vol. ii, fol. 93–94, 122–3, 125–6; vol. ix, fol. 168; vol. i, fol. 99, 112 *bis*.   [5] MA 152.

printing in this type to our knowledge is of 1683 (408, 410). The letters are respectably cut, but the fount is spoiled by the poor drawing and exaggerated curls of the capital letters.

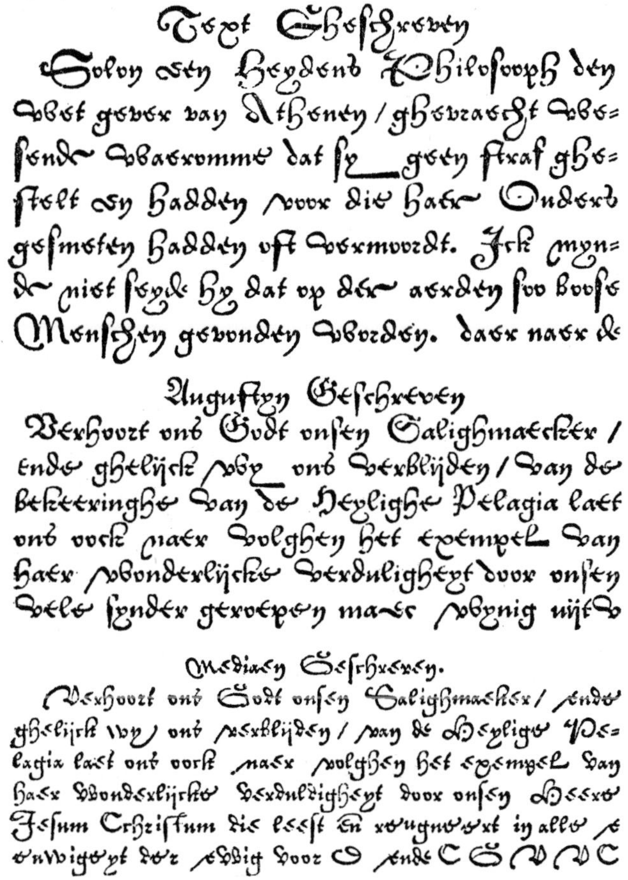
Text Geschreven
Solon een Heydens Philosooph den
wel gever van Athenen / ghevraecht we-
sende waeromme dat sy geen straf ghestelt en hadden voor die haer Ouders
gesmeten hadden oft vermoordt. Ick meyn-
de niet seyde hy dat op der aerden soo boose
Menschen gevonden worden. daer naer de

Augustyn Geschreven
Verhoort ons Godt onsen Salighmaecker /
ende ghelijck wy ons verblijden / van de
bekeeringhe van de Heylighe Pelagia laet
ons oock naer volghen het exempel van
haer wonderlijcke verduldigheyt door onsen
vele synder geroepen maer weynig uyt-

Mediaen Geschreven.
Verhoort ons Godt onsen Salighmaecker / ende
ghelijck wy ons verblijden / van de Heylige Pelagia laet ons oock naer volghen het exempel van
haer wonderlijcke verduldigheyt door onsen Heere
Jesum Christum die leeft en regneert in alle e-
ewigheyt der ewig voor O ende C G V V C

FIG. 40. Civilité types in a specimen by the typefounder Melchior van Wolsschaten, Antwerp, *c.* 1710. Types E1, E2, E3.

E2. *Van Wolsschaten's Augustyn* (fig. 40)

The second script in the same specimen, headed 'Augustyn Geschreven', is on the body equivalent to our English. The lower case is the Paragon of Tavernier (C1, above) with smaller ascending and descending letters cut to fit this body, and the capitals are an alphabet of *Fraktur* considerably too big.

The remodelling of Tavernier's Paragon to make it fit on a smaller body goes back to the sixteenth century. An example is found at

Louvain in 1601 (291), where the capitals of Granjon's *St. Augustin* are matched with the reformed lower case, and in 1603 the mixture appeared at Antwerp (296, 297). Later an ill-assorted set of capitals, some of a provenance unknown to us, was substituted in books printed at Antwerp from 1635 (373) until the nineteenth century (617), making a mixture which we have designated E2a (fig. 42). The *Fraktur* capitals put with the fount in the specimen by Van Wolsschaten occur with it in a book of 1683 (409).

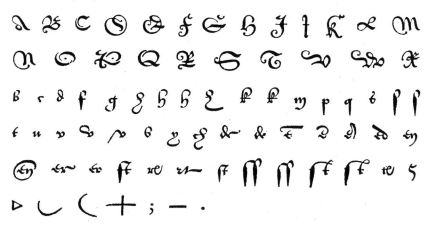

FIG. 41. The characters of the Paragon Gheschreven of Van Wolsschaten cast in the incomplete set of matrices at the Museum Plantin-Moretus. Type E1.

These extemporized founts are probably to be explained by a desire for a Gothic script of distinctively Flemish style intermediate in size between the two that Tavernier bequeathed to his countrymen.

E3. *Van Wolsschaten's Mediaen* (fig. 40)

The third type offered in the specimen, on a Pica body, is to be seen in a book printed at Antwerp in 1672 (397), and it became a common type in the printing of the southern Netherlands.

The impressions from this face that we have seen are so rough (and this includes the founder's specimen) that we cannot tell whether it was an original work or a mixture of the older types by Tavernier (C2) and Van den Keere (D1).

F. THOMAS COTTRELL'S 'ENGROSSING' (fig. 43)

This type for the law-hand written in England in the latter part of the eighteenth century preserves the essential character of the Secretary, though some letters, S E Q, are assimilated to Italic. Cottrell set up as a typefounder in London in 1759.[1] The type, which he named 'Engrossing', appears in several of his undated specimens[2] and in P. Luckombe's *History and Art of Printing*, 1771.

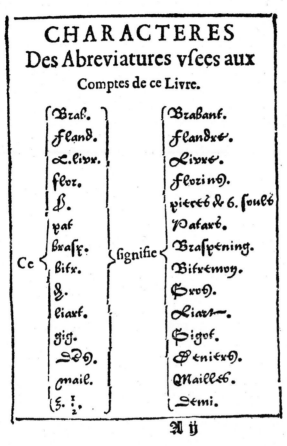

FIG. 42. A page of R. van Heusden, *Livre de comptes*, Antwerp, J. Trognesius, 1635. Type E2a, Van Wolsschaten's *Augustyn* with capitals from various sources.

A leaflet issued by William Richardson, printer, displaying the type, was known to Talbot Baines Reed, and in it Richardson claimed to have provided the model and recommended the face as 'proper for

[1] T. B. Reed, *A History of the Old English Letter Foundries*, ed. A. F. Johnson (London, 1952), p. 290.

[2] W. T. Berry and A. F. Johnson, *Catalogue of Specimens of Printing Types by English and Scottish Printers and Founders, 1665–1830* (London, 1935), pp. 32–36.

And be it further hereby enact
ed, That the Mayors, Baili=
ffs, or other head Officers of eo
ery Town and place corporate,
and City within this Realm
being Justice or Justices of P
eace, shall have the same au=
thority by virtue of this Act,
within the limits and precincts
of their Jurisdictions, as well
out of Sessions, as at their Sess=
ions, if they hold any, as is he=
rein limited, prescribed and ap=
pointed to Justices of the Pea
A B C D E F G H I J K =
L M N O P Q R S T U V

FIG. 43. Thomas Cottrell's Engrossing type in his *Specimen of Printing Types*, London,
[*c.* 1768]. Type F1.

N^o. L V.

CIVILITÉ

CORPS DE GROS-ROMAIN.

*L'éducation de la Jeunesse est assu-
rément de la dernière conséquence; ainsi
Pere & Mere Vous Voyez l'obligation
indispensable que Vous avez de prendre un
très-grand soin de vos enfans : faites
leur prendre de bonnes habitudes; instrui-
sez-les pendant qu'ils sont jeunes ; éle-
vez-les en la crainte de Dieu, portez-les
à s'acquitter de leur devoir envers
leur prochain; faites-leur apprendre les re-
gles de la bienséance & faites-les leur
pratiquer ; ne leur laissez rien passer
quand ils manquent.*

M. ROSART, fils, sculp.

M. ROSART, fils, sculp.

FIG. 44. The Gros Romain Civilité type of Matthieu Rosart in *Épreuves des caractères de J. L. de Boubers*, Brussels, 1777, and, at the foot, the lower-case alphabet adapted for the body of *St. Augustin*. Type G1.

leases, agreements, indentures, etc.'[1] The matrices for this '2-line English Engrossing' now belong to Messrs. Stephenson, Blake & Co. Ltd., of Sheffield.

G1. A CIVILITÉ TYPE BY MATTHIAS ROSART (fig. 44)

The typefounder Jean Louis de Boubers of Brussels put in his book of *Épreuves* dated in 1777 two Civilité types of typically French design, a *Gros texte* (Great Primer) and a *St. Augustin* (English), with the legend under each of them 'M. Rosart fils sculp.' There is only one face on the two bodies, apart from some flourished sorts which would not come on the smaller one.

Matthias, son of the better-known punchcutter Jacques François Rosart, cut a good many types for De Boubers and some for Johannes Enschedé.[2] His aesthetic judgement was less than his skill. His Civilité lacks the true cursive rhythm. On the whole the design follows Granjon's, but there are some letters like Danfrie's first type of the kind.

Rosart's Civilité is to be found in a book printed at Ghent in 1768 (506), and it is not uncommon in Belgian and French printing of the nineteenth century.

H. GOTHIC SCRIPT TYPES BY UNKNOWN PUNCHCUTTERS

H1. *A Civilité Type used at Ghent* (fig. 45)

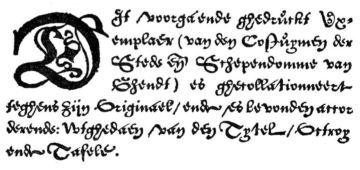

FIG. 45. A paragraph of *Costumen der Stede van Ghent*, Ghent, H. van den Keere, 1564. Type H1, a Flemish type of unknown origin.

A type for the heavy Germanic fashion of cursive script, much like the *Parangon* of Tavernier, was used by Hendrik van den Keere the Elder at Ghent to print three ordinances for the city. The two earlier were promulgated in 1563, so the undated printed pamphlets would be

---

[1] T. B. Reed, *A History of the Old English Letter Foundries* (London, 1887), pp. 289–90. The leaflet has since disappeared.   [2] Enschedé, *Fonderies*, pp. 266–70.

of about that time (70, 71), and the third (84) is dated 1564. In 1567 Gheerart van Salenson, bookseller of Ghent, made use of a fount of the same type (109).

The printer of the ordinances was not the punchcutter responsible for a type previously described (D1), but his father of the same names. In 1553 the father of the elder Van den Keere had bought the house opposite the town hall where Joos Lambrecht had been in business as printer and typefounder.[1]

In the ordinances the face is cast on the *Augustijn* (English) body, which is too small for it, so that the page looks crowded. More than a century later the type-face reappears in an undated specimen-sheet of the widow of Dirk Voskens, typefounder of Amsterdam, with the *Mediane geschreven* of the younger Van den Keere.[2] The larger face is there cast on the body of Great Primer and headed 'Text Gheschreven'. The specimen dates from the period 1690–1715. Both faces can be found in Dutch books until 1857 (633). It is a type of archaic appearance representing the Flemish cursive hand in a form that seems old-fashioned for 1563.

H2. *The English Great Primer Secretary* (figs. 13, 46)

Attempts to discover the origin of this face have been unavailing.[3] In all likelihood it is the one for which Henry Bynneman had matrices in 1583.[4] Matrices, but not punches, belonged to the London typefounder John James at the time of his death in 1773, and 114 of them were Lot 78 in the Sale of his foundry in 1782.[5] Rowe Mores thought they had been in the typefoundry of Grover;[6] but his lists suggest that the lot sold in 1782 was a relic of a combination of 105 matrices from Grover with 15 for capitals from the foundry of Robert Andrews.[7] After 1782 there is no trace of them.

We know of nothing printed in this face after 1613 (341). It probably looked old-fashioned by then and was superseded by the type we refer to as H7.

---

[1] F. Vanderhaeghen, *Bibliographie gantoise*, i (Ghent, 1858), pp. 56, 160.

[2] B.M. Harl. 5930, No. 541, reproduced in *Type Specimen Facsimiles*, ed. John Dreyfus (London, 1963), No. 8.

[3] A. F. Johnson, *Type Designs* (London, 1959), pp. 141–3.

[4] See pp. 37–38.

[5] Edward Rowe Mores, *A Dissertation upon English Typographical Founders and Founderies*, ed. H. Carter and C. B. Ricks (London, 1961), fourth page of 'A Catalogue and Specimen' following p. 104.

[6] Ibid., p. 46.

[7] Ibid., p. 47.

Trusſie and welbeloued, wee greete you well : &
our subiects the leaſt doubt of our vnwillingnes
deſire to auoide it in the whole courſe of our gouernme
vpon vs (in no ſort to be eſchewed) as wee ſhall be
meante, or to want without great preiudice.   In wo
how much wee found the Crowne exhauſted by the acci
of our dayly expence euer ſince wee came into this Ki
that as our neceſſitie is the onely cauſe of our Requeſt,
may further adde one thing, which is no leſſe notori
hath beene affourded vs, notwithſtanding more extra
euer lighted vpon any King of this Realme.   & ma
ſeruice and fidelitie in the higheſt pointes wee haue ha
fourme of Subſidies offered to Princes in Parlian

FIG. 46. A form of demand for a forced loan, [London, 1604] (part). Type H2, the
English Great Primer Secretary type.

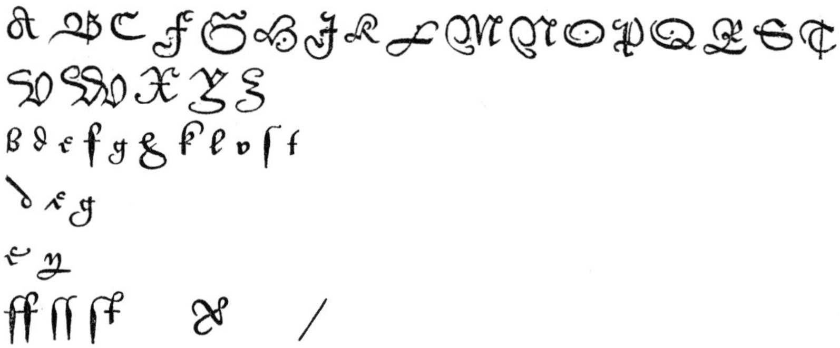

A B C F G H I K L M N O P Q R S T
V W X Y Z
B d e f g g k l v ſ ſt
d r g
e y
ff ſſ ſt & /

FIG. 47. The characters of Type No. 9 of Joh. Enschedé en Zonen. Type H3.

EN ANVERS,
Chez Henry Heyndricx, sur le Cemitiere nostre Dame/
a la fleur De Lis.

1576.

FIG. 48. The imprint of Henry Heyndricx in *Nouvel ABC*, Antwerp, 1576. Type H3.

H3. *A Type used by Henry Heyndrickx* (figs. 47, 48)

The Antwerp printer of this name set his imprint in a book of 1576 (141) in a Great Primer Civilité of Flemish style which we have not seen elsewhere.

Fifteen of the sorts occurring in this imprint have been preserved in a set of matrices belonging to Messrs. Enschedé of Haarlem—No. 9 in their inventory. The matrices for this curious assortment of letters are said to have been bought by Johannes Enschedé in 1767 from the brothers Ploos van Amstel of Amsterdam.[1] The set is not complete, but the matrices are uniform, evidently made by one workman at one time, so that the difference in the size of the letters can be explained only by heterogeneity of the punches with which they were struck. Nine of the capitals and nine lower-case letters are evidently meant for Double Pica body, while the rest are of the right gauge for Great Primer. How and why the mixture happened are unanswerable questions. The ascription of the resulting face to Ameet Tavernier[2] appears to be recent and not maintainable. In 1768 Johannes Enschedé showed it in his *Proef van Letteren* (508) headed simply 'Text Oud Geschreeven'. The eighteen letters of the larger gauge do not occur in any printing that we have seen.

H4. *H. J. Muller's Civilité* (fig. 49)

Harmen Jansz. Muller, printer of Amsterdam, had begun by 1578 (154) to use a rather primitive Civilité type on the body of English (*Augustijn*). He was also an engraver on wood and in copper:[3] possibly, therefore, he cut this face himself. The type has been found only in Muller's printing, and its last occurrence known to us is in 1590 (257).

H5. *The Civilité Type of Soolmans* (figs. 50, 51)

Niclaes Soolmans, printer and bookseller at Antwerp, had two Civilité types, the *Mediane* of Van den Keere (D1, above), and another for English body whose origin we do not know. The second of these was used in a manual of accounting printed by Soolmans in 1582 (210). The type borrows a good many capitals from the *St. Augustin* of Granjon (A2), and some of the lower-case letters are common to this and the type we have numbered H3. The same blend of types was used by the printer Abraham vanden Rade at Leeuwarden (343, 344). Messrs. Enschedé have matrices for this face also—their No. 8.[4]

---

[1] Enschedé, *Fonderies*, pp. 42, 43.   [2] Ibid.

[3] E. W. Moes and C. P. Burger, *De Amsterdamsche Boekdrukkers en Uitgevers in de 16de. Eeuw*, (Amsterdam, 1900), pp. 285 ff.   [4] Enschedé, *Fonderies*, p. 40.

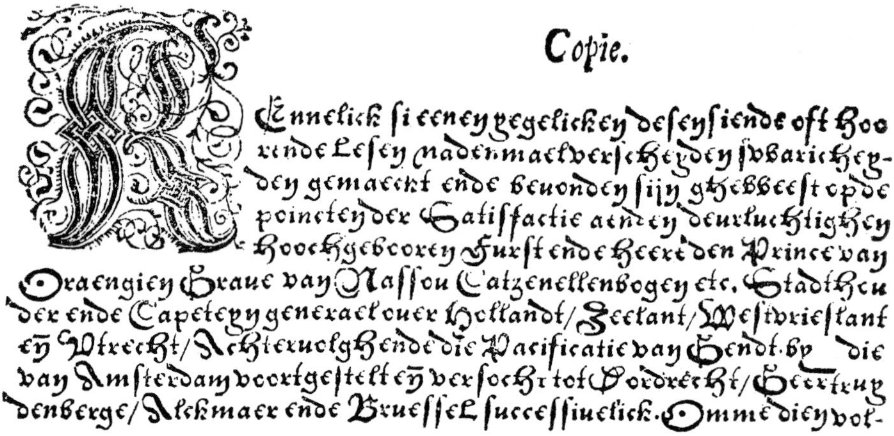

Copie.

[Blackletter/gothic facsimile text — FIG. 49]

FIG. 49. From *Poincten ende Articulen van de Satisfactie* &c., Amsterdam, H. J. Muller, 1578. Type H4.

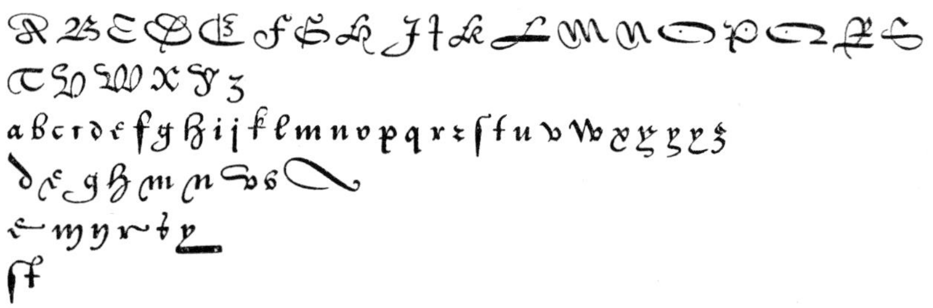

FIG. 50. The characters of Type No. 8 of Joh. Enschedé en Zonen. Type H5.

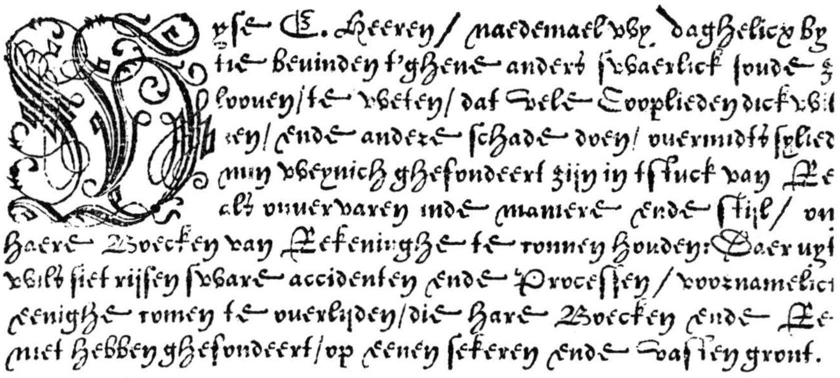

[Blackletter/gothic facsimile text — FIG. 51]

FIG. 51. From B. Cloot, *Corte Maniere om Boek te Houden*, Antwerp, N. Soolmans, 1582. Type H5.

Johannes Enschedé put the type in his specimen-book of 1768 (508) with the name of Ameet Tavernier beneath it (fig. 21): but there is no evidence (or, as we think, likelihood) that Tavernier had a hand in any of the constituents of this blend.

H6. *Aelbrecht Heyndricxzoon's Civilité* (fig. 52)

A book (225) was printed at Delft in 1584 by this printer in a Civilité type whose origin we do not know. It reappears at Rotterdam in 1590

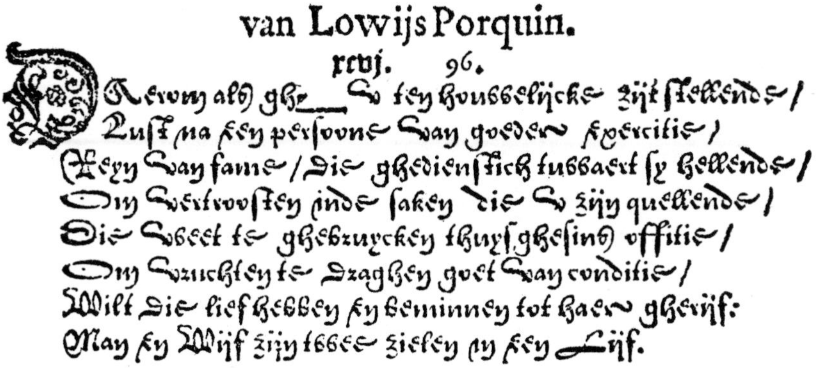

FIG. 52. From *Den wtersten Wille van Lowys Porquin*, Rotterdam, D. Mullem, c. 1590–95. Type H6.

(259), at Zwolle in 1607–8 (307), and at Arnhem in 1615 (346). It looks like a crude imitation of the 'Dutch' *St. Augustin* of Granjon (our A4).

H7. *The English Engrossing Secretary* (fig. 53)

This type for a body of Paragon was commonly used for law forms from about 1616 nearly until the end of the century.[1] It represents a distinctly English and late variety of the Secretary used by law clerks, a more formal hand than the running Secretary used for other business. An engraved model strikingly like the type is in *The Writing Schoole-Master* by John Davies of Hereford (d. 1618).[2] Nothing is known about punches or matrices for this face.

---

[1] A. F. Johnson, *Type Designs* (London, 1959), p. 143. We cannot trace a royal printed letter of 3 Jac. I there referred to. A contract between Hugh Myddelton and users of his London water-supply for 14 Jac. I (1616) is the earliest occurrence of the type for which we can vouch.

[2] S.T.C. 6345 (16th ed., 1636). The page is reproduced from an edition of 1663 by E. F. Strange, 'The Early English Writing Masters', *Bibliographica* 3 (London, 1897), at p. 165.

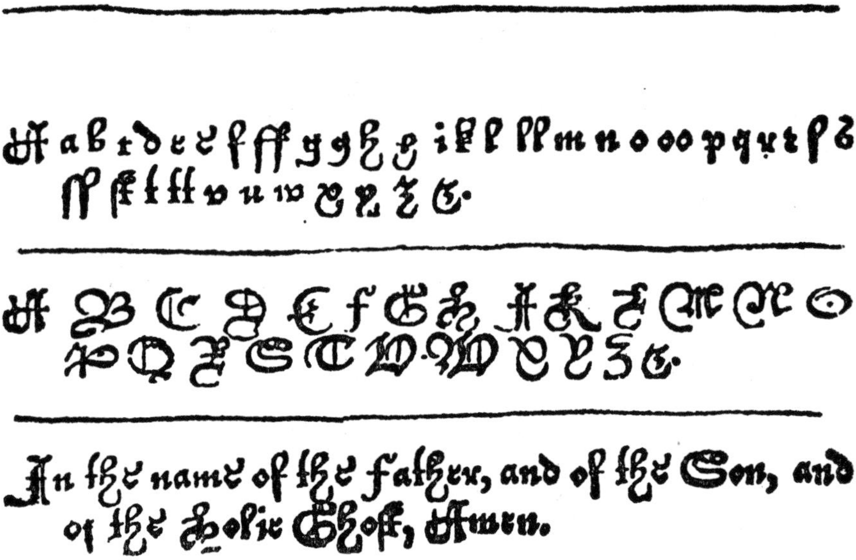

FIG. 53. A model for Secretary hand in Edmund Coote's *English School-Master*, 35th. edition, London, E. Tyler for the Company of Stationers, 1669. Type H7.

FIG. 54. From John Barnard's *First Book of Selected Church Musick*, London, E. Griffin, 1641. Type H8.

H8. *The Type of Barnard's Church Musick* (fig. 54)

The face, known only by its appearance in this one book (376), is like the Engrossing Secretary in design.

H9. *Enschedé's Bâtarde* (fig. 55)

We have noticed the use in Holland up to the middle of the seventeenth century of the Bastarde that Granjon sold to Plantin (A6, above). A face evidently copied from it is to be seen in a specimen printed at

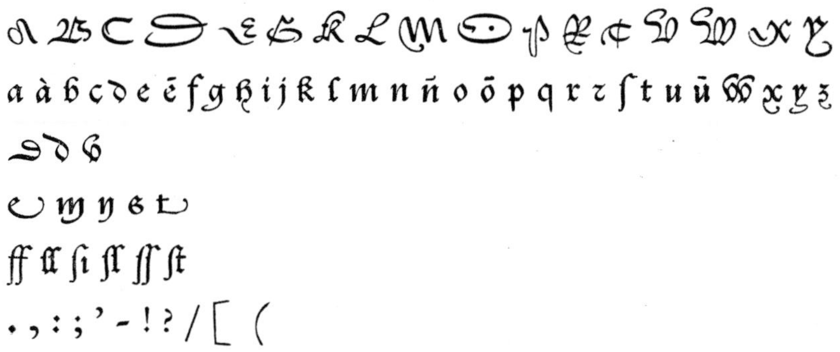

FIG. 55. The characters of Type No. 30 of Joh. Enschedé en Zonen. Type H9.

Amsterdam in 1653 (386*a*), and a fount of the type was offered at the sale of the effects of P. Boeyeszoon, printer of Hoorn in Holland, in 1692.[1] This face, described in the sale-catalogue as 'Text Geschreven', is very hard to tell apart from Granjon's, but it is slightly smaller and its capitals are not uniform, some being copies of the Bastarde and others much too small and of a different design. Matrices for this type, as it was shown in Boeyeszoon's specimen of 1682, belong to Messrs. Enschedé and are numbered 30 in their inventory.[2] According to Charles Enschedé, the matrices derive from the foundry of Anthonie and Hendrik Bruyn at Amsterdam, who showed the face in a specimen of about 1729 (445).

H10. *A Civilité at Angers* (fig. 56)

L. Pavie, a printer at Angers, produced three editions of the *Civilité puérile* in 1811–14 in a type closely resembling Breton's *Gros romain* (B2). We have at the time of writing noticed it only in Pavie's books 565, 571, 574).

---

[1] Enschedé, *Fonderies*, pp. 119–22. [2] Ibid.

ALPHABETS

De pluſieurs écritures, pour mieux
inſtruire les Enfans.

prononciation des lettres de l'Alphabet.

Lettres Romaines Capitales.

A, B, C, D, E, F, G, H, I, J, K, L, M,
N, O, P, Q, R, S, T, U, V, X, Y, Z.

Lettres Capitales Italiques.

A, B, C, D, E, F, G, H, I, J, K, L, M,
N, O, P, Q, R, S, T, U, V, X, Y, Z.

Lettres Françoiſes.

a, б, c, ꝺ, є, f, g, ꝉ, i, j, k, ſ, m, n,
v, p, q, r, ꞓ, ſ, t, u, ꝺ, ꝗ, ꝫ, ꝫ.

Capitales.

N, ꝯ, Є, Ꝺ, Ꝫ, f, Ꝺ, ꝉ, Ꝫ, k,
Ꝉ, ꝳ, ꝳ, Ꝺ, Ꝫ, Q, Ꝛ, Ꝫ, Ꝭ,
Ꝭ, Ꝫ, Ꝭ, Ꝭ, Ꝫ.

Six Voyelles, a, є, i, v, u, ꝫ.

Dix-neuf Conſonnes.

б, c, ꝺ, f, ꝗ, ꝉ, k, ſ, m, n, p, ꝗ, r, ꞓ, t, v, ꝗ, ꝫ.
Є'eſt erreur que ꝺe prononcer бoi, cui,
ꝺoi, êfre, oꝗe, eſſe, en, me, Єt.

LARGE INITIAL LETTERS

We have mentioned incidentally some of the big capitals of the cursive Gothic fashion made to serve as ornamental initials with Civilité types. Some of them, Bynneman's for example,[1] were woodcuts, and without guidance from records it is unsafe to judge by the impression whether the letters were printed from type. It is on the whole unlikely that any exceeding the body of Canon (say 12 mm.) would have been cut in the sixteenth century on punches and cast in struck matrices. Bigger letters were cut in wood and duplicates, if they were needed, were moulded in sand.[2]

The initials were almost all imitations of pen-work (we know of only one book in which there are cursive Gothic letters cut in outline against a rectangular decorated background (fig. 30). The manuals of sixteenth-century writing masters provide plenty of examples. In these, as in printing, cursive forms were sometimes given to initials set to matter in formal Black Letter.

As we have said[3] matrices for some Civilité initials on 2-line Pica body by Ameet Tavernier are preserved at the Museum Plantin-Moretus.

Enschedé's Initials No. 10 (fig. 57)

Messrs. Enschedé have an incomplete set of matrices for 2-line Small Pica initials of the Secretary fashion, lacking F L X Y. It is of sixteenth-

FIG. 57. The characters of Type No. 10 of Joh. Enschedé en Zonen.

century date, for the A is recognizable in a book printed by Willem Silvius at Antwerp in 1576 (142). Charles Enschedé found some of the letters in use by Aelbrecht Heyndricxzoon at The Hague in 1588 with a text in Black Letter.[4]

---

[1] See p. 38.

[2] The accounts of Hendrik van den Keere with Plantin for 1577 contain items for casting four 'alphabets de Cadeaulx, 96 pieces' and for making boxes to hold 'poinsons de ... Cadeaux en bois': MPM, Arch., vol. 42, fol. 13–13ᵛ.

[3] See p. 69.   [4] Enschedé, *Fonderies*, pp. 43, 47.

TABLE I. *The Civilité Types in Order of Date*

Earliest date	Description	Cutter	Depth of 20 lines in mm.	Carter–Vervliet No.	Punches or matrices preserved at
1557	Mediane	Granjon	80	A1	MPM: MA 38, MA 107
1558	Breton's Gros Canon	Danfrie (?)	c. 310		sandcast?
1558	Breton's Petit petit Canon	Danfrie (?)	c. 170		sandcast?
1558	Breton's St. Augustin	Danfrie	105	B1	Deberny-Peignot, Civilité No. 5
1559	Petite Parangonne	Tavernier	120	C1	MPM: MA 163
1560	Mediane	Tavernier	80	C2	
1561	Hamon's Petite Augustine françoise	Danfrie (?)	85	B3	
c. 1562	St. Augustin	Granjon	94	A2	MPM: ST 46, MA 158
c. 1563	Ghent Text		100	H1	MPM: MA 138; Enschedé, Civ. No. 11
1565	Pré-Courante	Granjon	120	A3	
1566	Dutch St. Augustin	Granjon	96	A4	Enschedé, Civilité No. 13
c. 1566	Françoise sur la Garamonde	Granjon	65	A7	MPM: ST 48, MA 50
1567	Courante	Granjon	116	A5	MPM: ST 44, MA 108
1568	Bastarde	Granjon	116	A6	MPM: ST 45, MA 109
c. 1570	Mediane	Van den Keere	80	D1	MPM: ST 47; Enschedé, Civ. No. 14
bef. 1571	Breton's Gros Romain	Danfrie (?)	120	B2	
1576	Bynneman's English Secretary	—	110	H2	
1576	Heyndricx Petite Parangonne	—	120	H3	Enschedé, Civilité No. 9
1578	Muller's St. Augustin	—	88	H4	
1582	Soolmans' St. Augustin	—	96	H5	Enschedé, Civilité No. 8
1584	Heyndrickx' St. Augustin	—	94	H6	
1587	de Tournes' Petite Françoise	Granjon	67	A8	
1597	Gros Parangon Graphometre	Danfrie	140	B4	
1597	Parangon Graphometre	Danfrie	130	B5	
1601	St. Augustin	Wolsschaten	94	E2	
1616	English Engrossing	—	120	H7	
1641	Barnard's Engrossing	—	200	H8	
1653	Enschedé's Bâtarde	—	115	H9	Enschedé, Civilité No. 30
1675	Mediane	Wolsschaten	84	E3	
1683	Paragon	Wolsschaten	117	E1	MPM: MA 152
c. 1765	Engrossing	Cottrell	c. 180	F1	Stephenson Blake & Co.
1768	St. Augustin	Rosart	96	G1	
1811	Copy of Breton's Gros Romain	—	c. 120	H10	

TABLE 2. The Civilité Types classified by Size

Depth of 20 lines in mm.*	Description (or first user)	Cutter	Earliest date	Carter–Vervliet No.	Old names for the Body (French)	Old names for the Body (English)	Near equivalent in: Didot points	Near equivalent in: English points
c. 310	Breton's Gros Canon	Danfrie	1558	H8	Gros Canon	French Canon	41	44
200	Barnard's Engrossing	—	1641	F1	Petit Canon	3-line Pica	26·5	28
c. 180	Engrossing	Cottrell	c. 1765	—	Petit petit Canon	2-line English	24	25·5
c. 170	Breton's Petit petit Canon	Danfrie (?)	1558	B4	Petit petit Canon	2-line Pica	22·5	24
140	Gros Parangon Graphometre	Danfrie (?)	1597	B5	Gros Parangon	Double Pica	18·5	20
130	Paragon Graphometre	Danfrie	1597	C1	Parangon	Paragon	17·5	18·5
120†	Petite Parangonne	Tavernier	1558	B2	Gros Romain	Great Primer	16	17
120†	Breton's Gros Romain	Danfrie (?)	c. 1571	A3	"	"	16	17
120	Pré-Courante	Granjon	1565	H3	"	"	16	17
120	Heyndricx Petite Parangonne	—	1576	H4	"	"	16	17
120	English Engrossing	—	1616	H10	"	"	16	17
120	Copy of Breton's Gros Romain	—	1811	E1	"	"	16	17
117	Paragon gheschreven	Wolschaten	1683	A6	"	"	15·5	16·5
116	Bastarde	Granjon	1568	A5	"	"	15·5	16·5
116‡	Courante	Granjon	1567	H9	"	"	15·5	16·5
115	Enschedé's Bâtarde	—	1653	H2	"	"	15·5	16·5
110	Bynneman's English Secretary	—	1576	B1	St. Augustin	English	14·5	15·5
105	Breton's St. Augustin	Danfrie	1558	H1	"	"	14	15
100	Ghent Text gheschreven	—	1563	A4	"	"	13·5	14·5
96	Dutch St. Augustin	Granjon	1566	H5	"	"	12·8	13·7
96	Soolmans' St. Augustin	Granjon	1582	G1	"	"	12·8	13·7
94	St. Augustin	Rosart	1768	A2	"	"	12·8	13·7
94	St. Augustin	Granjon	c. 1562	H6	"	"	12·5	13·4
94	Heyndrickx St. Augustin	Wolschaten	1584	E2	"	"	12·5	13·4
94	St. Augustin	—	1601	H4	"	"	12·5	13·4
88†	Muller's St. Augustin	Wolschaten	1578		"	"	11·7	12·6
85	Hamon's Petite Augustine françoise	Danfrie	1561	B3	Mediane or Cicéro	Pica	11·2	12
84	Mediane	Granjon	1557	A1	"	"	11·2	12
84	Mediane	Wolschaten	1675	E3	"	"	11·2	12
80	Mediane	Tavernier	1560	C2	"	"	10·5	11
80†	Mediane	Van den Keere	c. 1570	D1	"	"	10·5	11
67	de Tournes' Petite françoise	Granjon	1587	A8	Petit Romain	Long Primer	9	9·5
65	Françoise sur la Garamonde	Granjon	c. 1566	A7	Garamonde	"	8·5	9

* The mm. measurement is approximate in the bigger sizes.

† Some characters in this face overhang the body.

‡ Though this face was rather smaller than the Bastarde (110 mm. in fact), it was cast for Plantin on the same body.

APPENDIX

A LIST OF BOOKS IN WHICH CIVILITÉ TYPES
ARE USED

THIS is a list of books that one or other of us has seen or, in a few instances, whose existence is vouched for by a named authority. The aim of our study being typographical rather than generally bibliographical, we have contented ourselves with a collection mainly from the British Museum, the Bibliothèque Nationale, the Bodleian Library, and the Museum Plantin-Moretus, certainly not exhaustive but wide enough, we believe, to bring to light all the type-faces of this description. We have excluded the books printed within the last hundred years or so, by Louis Perrin at Lyons and Joh. Enschedé en Zonen at Haarlem in which old Civilité types were used as archaisms.

The list is arranged chronologically and, within a given year, alphabetically by the place of publication.

The entries supply the author's surname and initial, a short title and imprint, and sometimes a reference to a bibliography. We have added the location of a copy or of several copies where they are to be found in the principal libraries, with shelf-marks if the items might be difficult to find in catalogues, and at the end a code-number for the type used. The code-numbers are used also in the text of our monograph and can be expanded by reference to the List of Contents or to the tables preceding this page. A plus-sign between two code-numbers indicates a mixture of the two type-faces.

The serial numbers at the beginnings of the items have been used for reference in the text. An asterisk * after one of them means that the book or job is mainly in Civilité type. The items not so marked contain small amounts of type of this kind.

Chronological order becomes increasingly difficult after the early part of the eighteenth century because the humble literature with which we are concerned thereafter was so often issued in undated editions. Where the printer is known we have given his undated books the earliest date at which he is known to have been active with the abbreviation p. for *post*. The dates so marked are not to be taken as our guess at the actual dates of the books; and in the case of dated editions we suggest that antedating is sometimes to be suspected. We have not attempted to distinguish different issues of undated books with the same title and set in the same type.

A key to the abbreviations is on pp. xiii, xiv.

1* Ringhieri, I. Dialogue de la vie et de la mort. *Lyons, R. Granjon*, 1557.   1557
Baudrier ii, 54. BN.   A1

2* [Ravillan, P. de.] L'ABC ou instruction chrestienne pour les petits   1558
enfants. *Antwerp, C. Plantin*, 1558. MPM.   A1

3* Beaulegue, B. Chansons nouvelles. *Lyons, R. Granjon*, 1558. Baudrier
ii, 56. BN.   A1

4* La Civilité, puerile distribuée par petitz chapitres [and Brunfels, O.]
De la discipline et institution des enfans. *Lyons, R. Granjon*, 1558.
Zurich.   A1

5* Des Periers, B. Les Nouvelles recreations. *Lyons, R. Granjon*, 1558.
Baudrier ii, 60. BM; BN; MPM.   A1

6* Galtherus, P. (Gautier de Châtillon). Alexandreidos libri decem. *Lyons,
R. Granjon*, 1558. Baudrier ii, 60. BM; Bodl.   A1

7* Horae in laudem beatissime virginis Marie. *Lyons, R. Granjon*, 1558.
Baudrier ii, 57. BM; BN.   A1

8* La Tour d'Albenas, B. de. L'Amie des amies. *Lyons, R. Granjon*, 1558.
Baudrier ii, 57. BM; BN; Bodl.   A1

9* La Tour d'Albenas, B. de. L'Amie rustique. *Lyons, R. Granjon*, 1558.
Baudrier ii, 59. BM; BN; Bodl.   A1

10* [Palaephatus.] Le Premier livre des narrations fabuleuses . . . trad. par
Guillaume Gueroult. *Lyons, R. Granjon*, 1558. Baudrier ii, 59, 60.
BM; BN; Bodl.; Brussels.   A1

11* Ringhieri, I. Dialogue de la vie et de la mort. *Lyons, R. Granjon*, 1558.
Bodl.   A1

12* [Corlieu, F. de (Veilroc).] Briefve instruction pour tous estatz. *Paris,
P. Danfrie & R. Breton*, 1558. BM; BN.   B1

13* Des Avenelles, P. Epitome ou abrégé des vies de 54 notables et excel-
lentes personnages . . . extrait du grec de Plutarque. *Paris, P. Danfrie
& R. Breton*, 1558. BM; BN; Bodl.   B1

14* [Gentillet, F.] Le Discours de la court. *Paris, P. Danfrie & R. Breton*,
1558. Rothschild i, 653. BN.   B1

15* Habert, F. Les Divins oracles de Zoroastre. *Paris, P. Danfrie & R.
Breton*, 1558. BM; BN.   B1

16 Ovid. Der Griecxser princerssen . . . Heroidum epistolae . . . [transl. by]   1559
Cornelis van Ghistele. *Antwerp, J. de Laet*, 1559. The Hague.   C1

17* [Erasmus, D.] Goede manierliicke seden. *Antwerp, J. van Waesberghe*,
1559. Rotterdam.   C1

18* Beaulaigue, B. Chansons nouvelles. *Lyons, R. Granjon*, 1559. BM;
BN.   A1

19* Beaulaigue, B. Mottez nouvellement mis en musicque. *Lyons, R. Granjon*, 1559. Baudrier ii, 62. BM; BN.   A1

20* [Domenichi, L.] Facecies. *Lyons, R. Granjon*, 1559. Baudrier ii, 61. BM; Bodl.; MPM.   A1

21* Le Premier trophée de musique. *Lyons, R. Granjon*, 1559. BM; BN. A1

22* Anacreon. Quelques odes d'Anacreon poete ancien...mises en musique par...R. Renvoysy. *Paris, R. Breton*, 1559. Paris, Arsenal. B1

23* Brief traicté de l'humilité, [transl. by] Gilb. Dert. *Paris, R. Breton*, 1559. BN.   B1

24* La Tapie d'Aurilhac, J. de. Préceptes nuptiaux de Plutarque. *Paris, R. Breton*, 1559. BN.   B1

25* Matthieu, A., sieur des Moystardières. Devis de la langue françoise. *Paris, R. Breton*, 1559. BN; Bodl.   B1

26* Plinius Secundus, C. Sommaire des singularitez de Pline, extrait par P. de Changy. *Paris, R. Breton*, 1559. BM.   B1

27* Le Soulas du cours naturel de l'homme, [transl. by] Gilb. Dert. *Paris, R. Breton*, 1559. BN.   B1

28* [Calviac, C. Hours de.] La Civile honesteté pour les enfants. *Paris, P. Danfrie & R. Breton*, 1559. Cf. J. Le Coultre, *M. Cordier*, p. 344. B1

29* [Corlieu, F. de (Veilroc).] Instruction pour tous estats. *Paris, P. Danfrie & R. Breton*, 1559. Rothschild i, 171. BM; BN; Bodl.   B1

30* [Habert, F.] La Premiere instruction pour les enfans...ensemble la maniere de prier Dieu en toutes necessitez. *Paris, P. Danfrie & R. Breton*, 1559. Wolfenbüttel, Herzog August.   B1

31* Les Quatre livres de Caton pour l'instruction de la jeunesse. *Paris, P. Danfrie & R. Breton*, 1559. BN.   B1

32* [Trissino, G.] Sophonisba, tragedie...[transl. by Mellin de Saint-Gelais]. *Paris, P. Danfrie & R. Breton*, 1559. Rothschild iv, 3057. BN.   B1

33* Union des sentences de philosophie. *Paris, P. Danfrie & R. Breton*, 1559. BM.   B1

34 Bibel, Den. *Antwerp, J. de Laet*, 1560. BM; MPM.   C1   1560

35 Sainctes, C. de. Liturgiae sive missae sanctorum patrum. *Antwerp, C. Plantin*, 1560. RDB 6. Bodl.; MPM.   A1

36* Gheestelycken, Eenen, ABC. *Antwerp, A. Tavernier*, [p. 1560]. Vervliet 3. Amsterdam.   C1

37* [Tredehan, P.] Le Trésor de la vertu. *Antwerp, [A. Tavernier for] J. Bellere*, 1560. Sabbe 4. MPM.   C1, 2.

38* Pseaumes de David mis en rhythme francoise par C. Marot et T. de de Besze. [*Geneva*,] *P. Davantes*, 1560. Amsterdam; BM; BN; Geneva.
A1

39 Pseaumes de David mis en rhythme francoise par Clement Marot et Theodore de Besze. [*Geneva*,] *Michel du Boys*, 1560. Cf. Pidoux, *Psautier huguenot* (Basle, 1962), ii, p. 118. Geneva.
A1

40* Augé, Daniel d'. Deux dialogues de l'invention poëtique de la vraie connoissance de l'histoire. *Paris, R. Breton*, 1560. BN.
B1

41* [Calviac, C. Hours de.] La Civile honesteté pour les enfans, avec la manière d'apprendre à bien lire, prononcer et escrire... *Paris, R. R. Breton*, 1560. BN.
B1

42* Matthieu, A., sieur des Moystardières. Second devis et principal propos de la langue françoise. *Paris, R. Breton*, 1560. BN; Bodl.
B1

43* [Trissino, G.] Sophonisba, tragedie... [transl. by Mellin de Saint-Gelais]. *Paris, R. Breton*, 1560. Tchemerzine, *Bibliogr. éditions orig. auteurs franç.* (Paris, 1933), x, 107.
B1

44 Magnus, Olaus [Månsson, O.] Histoire des pays septentrionaus. *Antwerp, C. Plantin*, 1561. RDB 11. MPM.
A1 1561

45* Aesop. Les Fables et la vie d'Esope. *Antwerp, A. Tavernier*, 1561. Vervliet 4. BM; Bodl.; The Hague, Mus. Meer.-Weest.
C1, 2

46 [Heyns, P.] Tot profijte van die willen leeren. *Antwerp, J. van Waesberghe* [1561]. BM. 8533. de. 20.
C1, 2

47 [Four poems contributed by the Chambers of Rhetoric of 's Hertogenbosch, Bergen op Zoom, and Berchem to the Landjuweel of 1561 at Antwerp.] *Antwerp*, s.n. Brussels II 13368 B–LP, fol. 15, 55, 56, 73.
C1, 2

48 [Calvin, J.] Catechismus latino-gallicus: le catechisme latin–françois. [*Geneva*,] *N. Barbier & T. Courteau*, 1561. Wolfenbüttel, Herzog August.
A1

49* [Corlieu, F. de.] Instruction pour tous estats. *Paris, R. Breton*, 1561. Sabbe & Audin 23. Edinburgh, Edw. Clark Memorial Library.
B1

50 Magnus, O. Histoire des pays septentrionaux. *Paris, Martin le Jeune*, 1561. (A reissue of No. 44 with a cancel title). BM; Oxford, New Coll.
A1

51 Hamon, P. L'Alphabet de linuention des lettres en diverses escritures. *Paris, J. Le Royer*, 1561. BM.
B3

52* Basile, St. Harangue de Saint Basile le Grand a ses ieunes disciples et neveux, trad.... par Claude de Pontoux... *Paris, J. Le Royer, P. Danfrie & P. Hamon*, 1561. BN.
B3

53* [Calvin, J.] Le formulaire ou la maniere d'instruire les Enfants en la chrestienté, fait en maniere de dialogue [*Paris, J. Le Royer, P. Danfrie et P. Hamon?*], 1561. Geneva.
B3

54 [Briaerde, L. de.] Tractaet ... van geschreven rechten ... bij L. de 1562
Royarde. *Antwerp, J. de Laet*, 1562. MPM. A1

55 Placcaet en ordinantie. *Antwerp, W. Silvius*, [1562]. BM. T. 1730 (1).
A1

56 Spelen van sinne vol scoone moralisacien ... *Antwerp, W. Silvius*,
1562. BM; MPM. A1

57 Spelen van sinne waerinne alle oirboirlijke ... *Antwerp, W. Silvius*,
1562. MPM. C1, 2

58* Een corte onderwysinghe wter heyligher schriftueren ... *Antwerp, A.
Tavernier*, 1562. Sabbe 9. Leyden. C1, 2

59* Forme et maniere de vivre des chrestiens en tous estats. *Lyons, R.
Granjon*, 1562. BM. A1+A2

60* Instruction chrestienne pour la jeunesse de France. *Lyons, R. Granjon*,
1562. BM; Lyons. A1+A2

61* Le Moyen de parvenir à la congnoissance de Dieu. *Lyons, R. Granjon*,
1562. BM. A1+A2

62* Reigle de vivre d'ung chascun chrestien. *Lyons, R. Granjon*, 1562.
BM; Paris, Arsenal. A1+A2

63* [Ringhieri, I.] Le Dialogue de la vie et de la mort, trad. par J. Louveau.
Lyons, A. Volant & T. de Straton, 1562. BN. A1

64* [Des Prez, F.] Recueil de la diversité des habits. *Paris, R. Breton*, 1562.
Bodl; Paris, Mazarine. B1

65 Mennher, V. Arithmetique ... *Antwerp, G. van Diest*, 1563. MPM. C2 1563

66 Meurier, G. Communications familieres. *Antwerp, P. van Keerberghe*,
1563. BM. C1

67 Ordonnancien, statuten ende maniere van procederen ... *Antwerp, W.
Silvius*, 1563. MPM. A2a

68 Remonstrances au Roy des deputez des trois estats de son duché de
Bourgoigne. *Antwerp, W. Silvius*, 1563. BM; Ghent. A2a

69* Porquin, L. Een lieflick memorie boeck. *Antwerp, A. Tavernier*,
1563. Sabbe 12. MPM. C1, 2

70* Ordinancie, statuut ende eeuwich edict nopende der coopmanschap,
stapel ende pryse van den aluynen. *Ghent, H. van den Keere*, [1563].
BM. H1

71 Ordinantie . . . zeevaert. *Ghent, J. van den Steene*, [c. 1563]. Vanderhaeghen i, 147. Ghent. H1

72 Calendier historial. *Lyons, J. de Tournes*, 1563. Bodl.; London, Victoria
& Albert Museum. A1

73* Reynaert de Vos. *Antwerp, [C. Plantin for] P. van Keerberghen,* 1564. 1564
Freiburg i. Br. A1

74* De Testamenten der XII patriarchen. *Antwerp, [C. Plantin for] P. van Keerberghen,* 1564. MPM. A1

75 Ovid. Der Griecxer princerssen ... Heroidum epistulae ... [transl. by Cornelis van Ghistele]. *Antwerp, J. de Laet,* 1564. Antwerp. C1

76 L'ABC, ou instruction pour les petis enfans, apres laquelle s'ensuit la civilite puerile, a laquelle auons adiousté la discipline et institution des enfans. *Antwerp, C. Plantin,* 1564. William H. Robinson, Ltd., Catalogue No. 62 (London, 1937), item 98. MPM, Arch. 3, fol. 5; 4, fol. 61; 36, fol. 70. A1

77* La Fontaine de la vie. *Antwerp, C. Plantin,* 1564. Rothschild v, 3209. BN; MPM. B3

78* Le Livre de l'Ecclesiastique. *Antwerp, C. Plantin,* 1564. RDB 26. MPM. B3

79* Statuten, articulen ende poincten, gheadviseert ende gheaccordeert ... in dese druckerye, ghenaemt den Gulden Passer. *Antwerp, C. Plantin* [1564]. MPM, Fol. Var. 1, f. 107–108; Fol. Var. 9, f. 2–3. A1

80* Coornhert, D.V. Eenen nieuwen ABC of materi-boeck, *Antwerp, W. Silvius,* 1564. Amsterdam. A2a

81* Crul, C. Eenen gheestelijcken ABC ghetogen wt den psalmen van David. *Antwerp, W. Silvius,* 1564. The Hague; MPM. A2a

82* Die Fonteyne des levens. *Antwerp, A. Tavernier,* 1564. Sabbe 15. Leyden. C1, 2

83 Hortulus animae. *Antwerp, A. Tavernier,* 1564. Vervliet 5. Brussels. C1, 2

84 Costumen der stede ... van Ghent. *Ghent, H. van den Keere,* 1564. Vanderhaeghen i, 192. Ghent. H1

85 De warachtighe geschiedenisse van alle gheloofweerdighe saken van ... Carolus de vijfste. *Ghent, G. van Salenson,* 1564. Vanderhaeghen i, 168. Antwerp; Ghent. C1, 2

86* La Civilité puérile. *Lyons, A. Volant & T. de Straton,* 1564. Sabbe & Audin pl. 6. A1

87* Vives, J. L. Introduction de philosophie divine. *Antwerp, [W. Silvius* 1565
for?] R. Granjon, 1565. Liège. A1+A2, A3

88 Den Bibel. *Antwerp, J. de Laet,* 1565. BM; MPM. C1

89 [Fruytiers J.] Ecclesiasticus. *Antwerp, W. Silvius,* 1565. MPM. A2a

90* Vives, J. L. Introduction de philosophie divine. *Antwerp, W. Silvius,* 1565. Sabbe & Audin 7. MPM. A2a

91 Een corte onderwijsinghe wter heyliger Schrifturen. *Antwerp, A.*
    Tavernier, 1565. Sabbe 20. MPM.   C1, 2

92 [Guevara, A. de.] Tgulden boeck van tleven ende seyndbrieven van ...
    Marcus Aurelius. *Antwerp, A. Tavernier,* 1565. Sabbe 16. MPM.   C1, 2

93* Union des sentences de philosophie. *Paris, R. Breton,* 1565. Rothschild
    v, 3376. BN.   B1

94 [Fabricius, G.] Elegantiarum puerilium ex Ciceronis epistolis libr. iii.   1566
    Antwerp, W. Silvius, 1566. MPM.   A4

95* Fruytiers, J. Het Leven der Roomsche ende Constantinopelsche key-
    seren int cort. *Antwerp, W. Silvius,* 1566. BM.   A2a

96* Aesop. Les Fables d'Esope. *Antwerp, A. Tavernier,* 1566. BM.   C1

97* Evangelien ende epistelen. *Antwerp, A. Tavernier,* 1566. Sabbe 23.
    Leyden.   C1, 2

98* Les Pseaumes mis en rime francoise par Clement Marot et T. de Bèze.
    [*Geneva,*] *T. Courteau for A. Vincent,* 1566. BM; Bodl.; Geneva. A1

99 [Petri, N.] Arithmetica. Praticque omme ... te leren chypheren.   1567
    Amsterdam, Widow of Jan Ewouts, 1567. Moes–Burger vi, 3, No. 506.
    Amsterdam.   A1

100 Index sive specimen characterum Christophori Plantini. *Antwerp, C.*
    Plantin, 1567. (cf. the facsimile reprint by D. McMurtrie, New York,
    1924). MPM.   A1, A5, B3

101 La Premiere et la seconde partie des dialogues francois. *Antwerp, C.*
    Plantin, 1567. MPM.   B3

102 Savonne, P. Instruction et maniere de tenir livres de comptes. *Antwerp.*
    C. Plantin, 1567. MPM.   A5

103* H., A. de [D. V. Coornhert, ?]. Nouvel exemplaire pour apprendre à
    escrire. *Antwerp, W. Silvius,* 1567. BM.   A2a, A4

104 Guicciardini, L. Description de tout le païs-bas. *Antwerp, W. Silvius,*
    1567. MPM.   A3, 4

105 Ordonnance et edict touchant le pris et valeur du florin. *Antwerp,*
    W. Silvius, 1567. Brussels II 6694-4°, No. 1.   A4

106 Ordonnancie der Co. Mat. verclarende met wat ghewicht den nieuwen
    gouden gulden. *Antwerp, W. Silvius,* 1567. Brussels II 6694-4°, No. 3.
                                                                         A4

107* Die Fonteyne des leuens. *Antwerp, A. Tavernier,* 1567. Sabbe 25.
    MPM.   C1, 2

108* Die Historie van den ouden Tobias. *Antwerp, A. Tavernier,* 1567.
    Sabbe 26. MPM.   C1, 2

109   Le Iardin d'armoiries. *Ghent, G. van Salenson,* 1567. Vanderhaeghen **i,**
       170. Ghent.   H1

110* [Des Prez, F.] Recueil de la diversité des habits. *Paris, R. Breton,*
       1567. BN.   B1

111* Les Quatre livres de Caton pour la doctrine de la jeunesse [ed. by
       F. Habert]. *Paris, R. Breton,* 1567. Rothschild v, 3376. BN.   B1

112* Heyns, P. ABC, oft exemplen. *Antwerp, C. Plantin,* 1568. BB i, XII,   1568
       H 52. MPM.   A5, 6, B3

113   [Heyns, P.] ABC, ou exemples propres. *Antwerp, C. Plantin,* 1568.
       Title-page only: MPM, Arch. 1228, f. 123ᵛ.   A6

114   L'Histoire de l'ancien Tobie. *Antwerp, C. Plantin,* 1568. Title-page
       only: MPM, Arch. 1228, f. 123ᵛ.   A6

115   Historie van den ouden Tobias. *Antwerp, C. Plantin,* 1568. Title-page
       only: MPM, Arch. 1228, f. 135.   A6

116   [Vesalius, A.] Anatomie. *Antwerp, C. Plantin,* 1568. BB i, XXV, V,
       103. RDB 41. MPM.   A6

117   Guicciardini, L. Description de tous le païs-bas. *Antwerp, W. Silvius,*
       1568. BM; MPM.   A3, 4

118* H., A. de [D. V. Coornhert?]. Nouuel exemplaire pour apprendre à
       escrire. *Antwerp, W. Silvius,* 1568. BM.   A1+A4

119* Hortulus animae. *Antwerp, A. Tavernier,* 1568. Vervliet 6. Louvain.
                                                                        C1, 2

120   Biblia sacra [polyglotta.] *Antwerp, C. Plantin,* 1569. RDB 1. MPM.   1569
                                                                        A5, 6, B3

121   [Estienne, R.] Traicté de la grammaire francoise. *Paris, R. Estienne*
       (II), 1569. BM; MPM.   B1

122   Ordinancie, edict ... op tstuck van de criminele iusticie ... *Antwerp,*   1570
       C. Plantin, 1570. RDB 27. MPM.   A5

123   Ordinancie, instructie oft onderwijs. *Antwerp, C. Plantin,* 1570.
       MPM, R 16. 23 (40).   B3

124* Ordonnantie ende wetten staende by elck werckende t'onderhouden.
       Antwerp, C. Plantin, [p. 1570–71]. MPM, Ex. 14(4).   A6

125* [Type-specimen.] Henric van den Keere de Jonghe, lettersteker,
       wenscht allen beminders van goeden letteren ... [*Ghent, H. van den
       Keere the younger, c.* 1570]. Sabbe & Audin pl. 18. MPM, Fol. Var. 1,
       f. 5a, Bm 40. 241 (3)   D1

126   Copie by den coninck. [*Antwerp, C. Plantin,* 1571?] MPM, R 16. 23   1571
       (42).   A5

127 Lumnius, J. F. Van dleven der christelijcker maechden. *Antwerp, C. Plantin*, 1571. RDB 23 MPM. B3

128 Placcaet . . . verbot ende interdictie van alle zilvere munte. *Antwerp, C. Plantin*, 1571. MPM, A 74 (4). A5

129* Henryson, T. Morall fabillis. *Edinburgh, T. Bassandyne*, 1571. Edinburgh. A1

129a Adriaensens, A. Van ghehoorsaemheyt . . . *Louvain, H. Welle*, 1571. Antwerp, Ruusbroec, 3114 G 14. D1

130* Ravisius, J. [J. Tixier de Ravisi.] Les Epitres moralles. *Antwerp, J. van Waesberghe*, 1572. BB i, XXI, R2. BM; Ghent. D1   1572

131* Union des sentences de philosophie. *Paris, Widow of R. Breton*, 1572. BN. B1

132 Guevara, A. de. Misprysinghe ende miserie des hoefs. *Antwerp*, [*G. Smits for*] *J. Bellere*, 1573. Ghent. C1, 2   1573

133 Le Quatrième livre d'Amadis de Gaule [transl. by N. de Herberay]. *Antwerp, W. Silvius*, 1573. MPM. A2a, 3, 4

134 Guevara, A. de. Misprysinghe ende miserie des hoefs. *Antwerp, G. Smits*, 1573. Ghent. C1, 2

135* [Habert, P.] Le Moyen de promptement et facilement apprendre en lettre françoise à bien lire, prononcer et escrire. *Paris, R. Granjon* [*c.* 1573]. BN. A2

136 Dale, J. vanden. De ure vande doot. *Antwerp, G. Smits*, 1574. BB i, VIII, D5. Brussels. C1   1574

137 Aubert, G. Hymne sur la venue du roy à monseigneur le grand prieur de France. s.l. [*Paris, R. Granjon?*], 1574. BN. A2

138 Deuchdelijcke solutien gesolueert bij vele ingenieuse componisten. *Antwerp, G. van den Rade*, 1575. MPM. D1   1575

139 The CL Psalmes of David. *Edinburgh, T. Bassandine*, 1575. STC 16580. Bodl., Mason CC84; Edinburgh. A1

140* James VI, king of Scotland. [Letter of the Privy Council dated 8.3.1575 ordering every parish to advance £5 for printing the Bible. *Edinburgh, T. Bassandyne*, 1575]. Edinburgh, MS. 3135. A1

141 Nouvel ABC. *Antwerp, H. Heyndricx*, 1576. MPM. H3   1576

142 Nicolay, N. de. Les Navigations, peregrinations et voyages faicts en la Turquie. *Antwerp, W. Silvius*, 1576. BM; MPM. A4

143 Nicolaï, N. de. Les Navigations, peregrinations et voyages faicts en la Turquie. *Antwerp, W. Silvius*, 1576, Sabbe & Audin, pl. 13. Bodl. A3, 4

144 Nicolaï, N. de. De schipvaert ende reysen. *Antwerp, W. Silvius*,
     1576.   A3, 4

145 Ordinancie ende ghebot beroerende den prijs ende weerde vandē gouden
     gulden. *Antwerp, W. Silvius*, 1576. MPM, R 16.23 (13).   A4

146 Guarna, A. Bellum grammaticale: the grammer warre. *London, H.
     Bynneman*, 1576. STC 12420. BM.   H2

147 [Thomas a Kempis.] Qui sequitur me, dat is die navolghinghe Christi.
     Louvain, J. Maes, 1576. Antwerp.   D1

148 Fauvre, A. Arithmetique familiere et succincte. *Paris, N. du Chemin*,
     1576. BN.   A2

149 Heyns, P. Spieghel der werelt. *Antwerp, C. Plantin*, 1577. RDB 15.   1577
     BB i, XII, H53. MPM.   A5

150 Houwaert, J. B. Milenus clachte. *Antwerp, [C. Plantin for] W. Silvius*,
     1577 [1578]. RDB 24. MPM.   A4, B3

151 Sommier discours des iustes causes ... contres ... Iehan d'Austrice.
     Antwerp, W. Silvius, 1577. MPM.   A4

152 Fruytiers, J. Corte beschrijvinghe van de strenghe belegheringhe ...
     der stadt Leyden. *Delft*, [s.n.], 1577. Amsterdam; MPM.   C2

153 Redenen ende curt verclaers waeromme het saisissement ... *Ghent*,
     Widow of P. de Clerck, 1577. Vanderhaeghen i, 530. MPM.   D1

154 Poincten ende articulen vanden satisfactie die van Aemstelredamme   1578
     gegeven. *Amsterdam, H. J. Muller*, 1578. Moes–Burger i, 296, No. 201.
     Amsterdam.   H4

155 Pointen ende articulen van den satisfactie die van Amstelredamme
     ghegheven. *Amsterdam, H. J. Muller*, 1578. Moes–Burger i, 296,
     No. 202. Amsterdam.   D1

156 Antwoorde van de generale staten. *Antwerp, C. Plantin*, 1578. RDB
     33. MPM.   A6

157* Oratie der ambassadeuren, vert. door J. B. Houwaert. *Antwerp, C.
     Plantin*, 1578. RDB 21; BB i, XII, H 29. MPM.   A5, 6

158 Ordinantie ... op de onderhoudenisse van de Pacificatie van Ghent.
     Antwerp, C. Plantin, 1578. RDB 35. MPM, A 75 (15).   A6

159 Placcaet ons sheeren des Conincx aangaende ... munte. *Antwerp, C.
     Plantin*, 1578. BM.   A5

160 Responce a vn petit livret ... du seigr. Don Iehan d'Autriche.
     Antwerp, C. Plantin, 1578. RDB 29. Antwerp; MPM.   A6

161 Responce veritable aux lettres patentes et persuasions abusives de ...
     Ian d'Austrice. *Antwerp, C. Plantin*, 1578. RDB 17. BM; MPM,
     R 16. 24 (4).   A6

162 Waerachtighe antwoorde op de opene brieven . . . van Don Jan van Oostenrijck. *Antwerp, C. Plantin,* 1578. RDB 18. BM; MPM, A 75 (6), A 1589 (4). A6

163* Houwaert, J. B. Milenus clachte. *Antwerp,* [*C. Plantin for*] *W. Silvius,* 1578. BM; Brussels. A4, 5, 6, B3

164 [Heere, L. de.] Beschryvinghe van . . . incōste des Princē vā Oraengien binnen der stede van Ghent, den xxix decembris 1577. *Ghent, Widow of P. de Clerck,* 1578. BB ii, XVI, H226; Vanderhaeghen i, 533. Ghent. D1

165 Rambaud, H. La Declaration des abus que l'on commet en escrivant. *Lyons, J. de Tournes,* 1578. Cartier 591. BM; Brussels. A2, 6

166 Les quatre livres de Caton pour la doctrine de la ieunesse. *Paris, Widow of N. du Chemin,* 1578. Title-page only. BM, Harl. 5922, No. 446. A2

167 [Heere, L. de.] Beschrijuinghe van . . . incomste . . . des Princen van Orangien binnen der stede van Ghent, den xxix decembris M. D. Lxxvij. s.l., s.n., 1578. BB ii, XVI, H 225. Ghent; MPM. C2

168 Brief der staten van Artois . . . tot . . . de generale staten van de Neder-   1579 landen. *Antwerp, C. Plantin,* 1579. RDB 38. BM; MPM, A 76 (1), R 16.27 (19). A6

169 Brief ende resolutie der staten . . . van Rijssel. *Antwerp, C. Plantin,* 1579. MPM, A 76 (6), R 16.27 (19). A6

170 Brieuen der keurvorsten die te Cuelen versamelt zijn. *Antwerp, C. Plantin,* 1579. RDB 58. MPM, R 16.27 (49). A5

171 Copie van eenen brief by den Prince van Parme. *Antwerp, C. Plantin,* 1579. RDB 40. MPM, A76 (2), R 16.27 (14). A6

172* [Form: Alsoo de Colonel . . . *Antwerp, C. Plantin,* 1579] MPM, R 16.27 (72), Fol. Var. i, f. 15. B3

173* [Forms: Taxes. *Antwerp, C. Plantin,* 1579] MPM, R 16.27 (54, 55, 78, 79, 80). A6

174 Heyns, P. Le miroir du monde. *Antwerp, C. Plantin,* 1579. BB i, XII, H55. Antwerp. A6

175 Houwaert, J. B. Declaratie van de triumphante incompst vanden Prince van Oraingnien. *Antwerp, C. Plantin,* 1579. RDB 36. MPM. A6

176 Houwaert, J. B. Sommare beschrijuinghe van de incomst van den aerts-hertoge Matthias. *Antwerp, C. Plantin,* 1579. BB i, XII, H30. RDB 35. BM; MPM. A5

177 Nieuwe ordonnancie op tstuck vande navigatie. *Antwerp, C. Plantin,* 1579. RDB 55. MPM, A 76 (8). A6

178 [Ordonnance] Anderwerf gheboden . . . opten 5.3.1579. [*Antwerp, C. Plantin,?*] 1579. MPM, R 16.27 (12). A6

179 Verbodt van niet te dienen. *Antwerp, C. Plantin,* 1579. RDB 48. MPM, R 16.27 (18), A 76 (4). A6

180 Vermaninghe gedaen door ... d'Artsch-Hertoge van Oostenrijck. *Antwerp, C. Plantin,* 1579. RDB 50. MPM, R 16.27 (20). A6

181 Noot, J. van der. Cort begryp der XII boeken Olympiades: Abregé des douze livres Olympiades. *Antwerp, G. vanden Rade,* 1579. Bodl.; MPM. D1

182 Traicté ... entre Montigny et ... La Motte. *Douai, I. Bogard,* 1579. MPM. C1

183 Declaratie der redenen ... om welcker wille de scepenē ... van Ghendt ... vernieut zijn. *Ghent, Widow of P. de Clerck,* 1579. Vanderhaeghen i, 546. MPM, R 16.27 (44). D1

184 Hille, C. van. Een christelick sermoen van de gheluck-saligheit. *Ghent, Widow of P. de Clerck,* 1579. BM. D1

185 Hille, C. van. Den cleenen siecken troost. *Ghent, Widow of P. de Clerck,* 1579. BM. D1

186 Hille, C. van. Den siecken troost. *Ghent, Widow of P. de Clerck,* 1579. BM. D1

187 Openinghe ghedaen den drye leden ... van Ghendt. *Ghent, Widow of P. de Clerck,* 1579. Vanderhaeghen i, 547. MPM, R 16.27 (50). D1

188 Den troubel binnen Brugghe. *Ghent, Widow of P. de Clerck,* 1579. MPM, R 16.27 (35). D1

189 Cort verhael van den aenslag geschiedt in Irlandt, door sommighe weder spanninghe tegen Enghellant, dewelcke verslagen zijn gheweest in 1579. *London,* [printed abroad, s.n.], 1579. STC 14258. BM; MPM. C1

190 Justificatie des magistraets tot Leyden teghens de calumnien, terzake van de differenten ... [s.l., s.n.], 1579. MPM, R 16.27/5. D1

191* [Ordonnance 's-Hertogenbosch] Alsoo byden publicatie op 8 ... julio [1579] van wegen ... t shertogenbossche. [s.l., s.n., 1579] MPM, R 16.27 (41). D1

192* [Ordonnance 's-Hertogenbosch] Alsoo zeeckere alteratien. [s.l., s.n., 1579] MPM, R 16.27 (53). D1

193 Nieuwe moderatie ende ordonnantie opt stuck vande collectatie. 1580 *Antwerp, C. Plantin,* 1580. RDB 29. MPM, R 56.15 (39). A6

194 [Specimen of Plantin's types compiled about 1580. *Antwerp, C. Plantin, c.* 1580] MPM, Fol. Var. ix, f. 125–34. Partly reproduced as appendix to H. Carter's paper on Plantin's types in *Gedenkboek der Plantin-dagen* (Antwerp, 1955), in *De Gulden Passer* 34 (Antwerp, 1956), pp. 121–43, and in *The Library,* 5th ser., xi (1956), pp. 170–9. A2, 5, 6, B3

195 De historie vanden ouden Tobias. *Antwerp, N. Soolmans,* 1580.
MPM.   D1

196 Coolhaes, C. Breeder bericht van die scheuringhe der kercken Christi
tot Leyden. [s.l., s.n.] 1580. Moes–Burger iv, 3, No. 603. MPM, R
16.30 (5).   D1

197 Helmduyn, H. J. Rekenboeck. *Amsterdam, Corn. Claesz.* [p. 1581].   1581
Amsterdam.   D1

198 Heuiter, P. de. Nederduitse orthographie. *Antwerp, C. Plantin,* 1581.
MPM.   A2, 5

199 Lobel, M. de. Kruydtboeck. *Antwerp, C. Plantin,* 1581. RDB 33.
MPM.   A6

200 Refereynen. *Delft, A. Heyndricxz,* 1581. BB i, XX, R 36. Ghent. D1

201 [Papius, A.] Ernesto comiti Palatino Rheni . . . Leodiensium episcopo
& principi inauguratio. *Liège, G. Morberius,* 1581. MPM, Fol. Var. i,
f. 12.   A2

202 Guichard, C. Funerailles et diverses manieres d'ensevelir des Rom-
mains, Grecs. . . . *Lyons, J. de Tournes,* 1581. Cartier 616. BM; Geneva.
A6

203 Savonne, P. Instruction et maniere de tenir lirues de compte. *Lyons, J.
de Tournes,* 1581. Cartier 625. MPM.   A6

204 Coustumes generales des pays et duché de Bretagne. *Rennes, J. du Clos,*
1581. BN.   B1

205 Coornhert, D. V. Van des menschen natuerlijcke vleesch wonder-
sproock. [s.l., s.n., 1581]. Moes–Burger i, 298; BB i, VI, PC 76;
Laceulle-vande Kerk, 80–83. Leyden.   A1

206 Coornhert, D. V. Tweeling vanden bruydt Christi. *Amsterdam, H. J.*   1582
Muller, 1582. Moes–Burger i, 299, No. 205; BB i, VI, C 112. BM;
Ghent.   A1

207 Coornhert, D. V. Lied-boeck. *Amsterdam,* [s.n., p. 1582.] Moes–Burger
i, 328, No. 243; BB i, VI, C 72. BM; Ghent.   A1

208* Houwaert, J. B. Pegasides pleyn. *Antwerp, C. Plantin,* 1582/3. BB i,
XII, H 15. BM; MPM.   A5, 6

209 Stevin, S. Tafelen van interest. *Antwerp, C. Plantin,* 1582. RDB 51;
BB i, XXIII, S 124. MPM.   A6

210 Cloot, B. Corte maniere om boeck te houden. *Antwerp, N. Soolmans,*
1582. Breda, Gemeente-Archief.   H5

211 [Cordier, M.] Le Miroir des escoliers. *Paris, L. Cavellat,* 1582. Paris,
Coll. Scheler.   A2

212* La Civilité puerile. *Paris, M. du Bois for C. Micard,* 1582. See
Livres d'enfance, Catalogue Gumuchian xiii (Paris, 1930), item
1754.   B1

213   Bret, J. Christelijcke seyntbrieuen. [s.l., s.n.] 1582. BB i, III, B 187. Ghent. C_2

214* Houwaert, J. B. De vier wterste. *Antwerp, C. Plantin*, 1583. RDB 28;   1583
      BB i, XII, H 19. BM; MPM. A_5, 6

215   Keuren der stadt Leyden. [*Leyden, J. van Hout*], 1583. Leyden. A_6, D_1

216* Form of indenture of grant by Queen Elizabeth I and Sir W. Raleigh of licence to trade in wines. *London*, [s.n., *c.* 1583]. London, PRO. See *Trans. Bibliogr. Soc.* xiii (1916), p. VI. H_2

217   Châtillon, J. de. Ordonnances de . . . Montpensier. *Lyons, J. de Tournes*, 1583. BN. A_5

218   Du Chesne, J. La Morocosmie. *Lyons, J. de Tournes*, 1583. Cartier 638. BN. A_2, 6.

219* [Andrelini, P. F.] Cent quatraines contenant les distiques latins de feu Mons. Fauste, en son vivant excellent poète de France. *Paris, L. Cavellat*, 1583. Paris, Arsenal. A_2

220* [Du Faur, G.] Les Quatrains du seigneur de Pybrac. *Paris, L. Cavellat*, 1583. Paris, Arsenal. A_2

221   Du Verdier, A. La Biographie et prosopographie des rois de France. *Paris, L. Cavellat*, 1583. London, Victoria & Albert Museum. A_2

222* Les Quatre livres de Caton pour la doctrine de la jeunesse [ed. by F. Habert]. *Paris, L. Cavellat*, 1583. Paris, Arsenal. A_2

223   Union des sentences de philosophie. *Paris, L. Cavellat*, 1583. Paris, Arsenal. A_2

224   De historie vanden ouden Tobias: L'Histoire de l'ancien Tobie.   1584
      Antwerp, [*M. de Rische for*] *N. Soolmans*, 1584. Paris, Mazarine. C_1, 2

225   Remonstratie by forme van discours aen allen . . . inhoudende 't epitaphium op de doot des . . . Heern Wilhelms . . . van Oraignien. *Delft, A. Heyndricxz.*, 1584. Antwerp, K 11190 (2). H_6

226   Bèze, T. de. De francicae linguae recta pronunciatione. *Geneva, E. Vignon*, 1584. Bodl.; Geneva; MPM. A_1

227   Twe-spraack vande nederduitsche letterkunst. *Leyden, C. Plantin*, 1584. RDB 7; BB i, XXIV, T16. MPM. A_6

228   Waghenaer, L. Jansz. Spieghel der zeevaerdt. *Leyden, C. Plantin*, 1584–5. Bodl.; Part I only MPM. A_5

229* Distiques de Caton pour les bonnes moeurs nouvellement traduicts de latine en ryme françois . . . par E. du Tronchet. *Paris, L. Cavellat*, 1584. Paris, Arsenal. A_2

230* Sulpitius, J. Des Bonnes mœurs et honnestes contenances que doit garder un ieune homme . . . œuvre composé premièrement en latin par Jean Sulpice de Sainct Alban dit Verulan et nouvellement tourné et trad. en rime françoise par paraphrase par Pierre Broe. *Paris, L. Cavellat*, 1584. Paris, Arsenal. A2

231 Verhael van de rechte middelen om soo wel den stand van de ghemeyne saecke als de religie in den Nederlanden te moghen behouden. [s.l., s.n., *Leyden, C. Plantin?*] 1584. MPM. A6

232 Colen, L. van. Kort claar bewijs. *Amsterdam, H. J. Muller*, [1585]. 1585
Moes–Burger i, 301, No. 208. Amsterdam. A1, H4

233 Veer, A. de. De schrickelijcken gruwelijcken blixem. [s.l., s.d. *Amsterdam, H. J. Muller*, 1585.] Moes–Burger, iii. 229, No. 443. Ghent. A1, H4

234* Het beclach van Antwerpen. *Antwerp, M. de Rische*, 1585. Antwerp. C1

235 [Furmerius, B.] Recht gebruyck ende misbruyck van tydlycke have [transl. by D. V. Coornhert]. *Leyden, C. Plantin*, 1585. RDB 7; 7; BB i, VI, C 57. BM; MPM. A5, 6

236 Haeyen, A. Amstelredamsche zee-carten. *Leyden, C. Plantin*, 1585. MPM. A6

236a Waghenaer, L. Jansz. Spieghel der zeevaerdt; eerste deel. *Leyden, C. Plantin*, 1585. BM. A5

237 Placcaet ende eeuwich edict . . . aengaende de vercoopinghen . . der gheestelijcke persoonen. *Louvain, J. Maes*, 1585. MPM, B 3572. D1

238* Du Val, P. Psalme par quatrains de la puissance & bonté de Dieu. *Paris, C. Micart*, [1585?]. BM. B1, 2

239 Manuael ofte handtboeck, inhoudende de weerde van den marck . . . 1586
Amsterdam, C. Claesz. [1586]. BM. C2

240 Colen, L. van. Proefsteen ende claerder wederleggingh. *Amsterdam, H. J. Muller*, 1586. Moes–Burger, i. 301, No. 209. Amsterdam. A1

241 Publicatie opt stuck vander munten. *Antwerp, W. van Parijs*, [1586]. Brussels, II 6694–4°, No. 5. D1

242* [Cordier, M.] Le Miroir des écoliers et pareillement aussi de toute la jeunesse. *Paris, L. Cavellat*, 1586. Paris, Arsenal. A2

243 [Coornhert, D. V.] Boeven-tucht. *Amsterdam, H. J. Muller*, 1587. 1587
BB i, VI, C 41; Moes–Burger i, 304–5, No. 213. Leyden. A1

244 La Plaisante histoire du noble et vaillant chevalier Pierre de Provence. *Antwerp, J. van Waesberghen*, 1587. Van Heurck No. 59. MPM. D1

245 Copie van sekere brieven door eenighe soldaten omtrent loenen op de Veluwe opghenommen. *Arnhem, W. Jansz. van Campen*, 1587. BM, T. 1716 (22). A6

246 Aristotle. Problemes d'Aristote. *Geneva, J. de Tournes*, 1587. Cartier
     666. Geneva.   A8

247 Copien der vonnissen binnen der stadt Leyden. *Leyden, J. van
     Hout*, 1587. BM.   A4, 6

248 Vermaninge ende waerschouwinge van die vande gerechte der stadt
     Leyden . . . opten tienden decembris M.D. LXXXVIJ. *Leyden, [J. van
     Hout]* 1587. MPM.   A4, 6.

249 Verantwoordinge vanden welgeboren heere Philips grave van
     Hohenloe . . . teghens zekere vertoogh . . . bij den grave van Leycester.
     Leyden, F. Raphelengius, 1587. Antwerp; MPM.   A6

250 Vermaninge ende waerschouwinge . . . der stadt Leyden . . . iegens
     t'bouxken . . . van Jacob Valmaer. *Leyden, Raedthuys [J. van Hout]*,
     [1587]. BM; MPM.   A4, 6

251 Blockland de Montfort, C. Instruction methodique pour apprendre
     la musique practique. *Lyons, J. de Tournes*, 1587. Cartier 688. BM;
     BN.   A2, 6.

252 [La Noue, O. de.] Paradoxe par le sieur de Teligny. *[Geneva,] J. de*   1588
     Tournes, 1588. Cartier 677. MPM.   A2, 8

253 Savonne, P. Brieve instruction de tenir livres de raison ou de compte.
     [Geneva], J. de Tournes, 1588. Lyons.   A6

254 Die wonderlijcke groote Armada die zijns Magt. den Coninck van
     Spaenghien heeft toegerust op Enghelandt. *Ghent, H. van Salenson*,
     1588. Vanderhaeghen i, 693. BM.   C1

255* Porquin, L. Den utersten wille van Lowys Porquin. *Delft, A. Heyn-*   1589
     dricksz., 1589. BM.   D1

256* Porquin, L. Den wtersten wille van Lowijs Porquin . . . in dichte   1590
     ghestelt by Anthonius Verensis. *Amsterdam, L. Jacobszoon*, 1590.
     Moes–Burger ii, 252, No. 458. The Hague.   A4

257* Porquin, L. Den vvtersten vville van Lovvys Porqvin. *Amsterdam,*
     H. J. Muller, 1590. Moes–Burger i, 313, No. 221. Amsterdam.   H4

258 [Thuys, J.] Ars notariatus. *Antwerp, A. 'sConincx*, 1590. Antwerp.
                                                                      C1, A2

259* Porquin, L. Den wtersten wille. *Rotterdam, D. Mullem, [c. 1590–95?]*.
     Amsterdam.   H6

260 [Du Faur, G.] Les Quatrains du seigneur de Pybrac. *Rouen, G.
     L'Oyselet [c. 1590]*. Rothschild iv, 3184. BN.   A2

261 Les Mots dorez du grave et sage Caton . . . [ed. by F. Habert].
     Rouen, G. L'Oyselet [c. 1590]. Rothschild iv, 3168. BN.   A2

262 Petri, N. Praticque om te leeren rekenen. *Amsterdam, B. Adriaensz.*,   1591
     Moes–Burger iii, 13, No. 514. Amsterdam.   D1

263 Valcoock, D. A. Een nut ende profytelijck boecxken, genaemt den regel der duytsche schoolmeesters, die prochie kercken bedienen, nu eerst uytghegheven ende ghepractiseert door Dirck Adriaensz. Valcoock. *Amsterdam, L. Jacobszoon,* 1591. Moes–Burger ii, 265, No. 464. The Hague. A4, D1

264 Vivre, G. de. Lettres missives familieres. *Antwerp, [H. Swingen for] G. Janssens,* 1591. BB i, XXV, V 16. Brussels. D1

265* [Guevara, A. de.] Libro llamado menosprecio de corte. *Lyons, J. de Tournes,* 1591. Cartier 690. Bodl. A8

266 Adriani, H. Catholicke sermoonen. *Antwerp, H. Verdussen,* 1592. 1592 Ghent. A2+C1

267 Ordonnantie . . . stadt Leyden . . . opt copen ende vercopen van den turf. [*Leyden, J. van Hout,* 1592]. MPM, 2–86. A4, 6

268 [Opmeer, P. van.] Dat schip van patientie. *Antwerp, A. 'sConincx,* 1593 1593. MPM. A2+C1

269 Houwaert, J. B. Houwaerts moralisatie. *Brussels, J. Mommaert,* 1593. BB i, XII, H 33. Ghent. C1

270 Houwaert, J. B. Den willecomme. *Brussels, J. Mommaert,* 1593. BB i, XII, H 34. Brussels; Ghent. C1

271* England: Proclamations. Abuses used in the heawing, sawing, and measuring of timber. [*London,* s.n., 1593] BM, MS. Lansd. 161, No. 22. H2

272* Dale, J. vanden. Traite de l'heure de la mort. *Antwerp, G. Janssens,* 1594 1594. BB i, VIII, D 11. Brussels. A2+C2

273 Houwaert, J. B. Houwaerts moralisatie. *Brussels, J. Mommaert,* 1594. BM. C1

274* [Voort, J. vander.] Het leven en sterven ben ic ghenaemt. *Rotter-* 1595 *dam, D. Mullem* [c. 1595–97]. Rotterdam. D1

275* Iacobi, H. Gheneuchlijcke, eerlijcke ende profijtelijke propoosten. 1596 *Haarlem, G. Rooman,* 1596. Laceulle-vande Kerk 398. Amsterdam; The Hague. D1

276 Den lusthof van rethorica. *Leyden, F. Raphelengius,* 1596. MPM. A6

277 Jacobi H. Ghemeene seyndtbrieven. *Amsterdam, E. C. Muller,* 1597. 1597 Moes–Burger iv, 143, No. 630. Amsterdam. D1

278 [Voort, J. vander.] Het leven en sterven ben ick genaemt. *Dordrecht,* *P. Verhaghen,* 1597. Antwerp. D1

279 Ovid. Olympe ou metamorphose d'Ovide, [transl. by G. du Bartas. *Geneva*], *J. de Tournes,* 1597. Cartier 698. Geneva. A6

279*a* Ordonnantie vanden Staten van Hollant ende West-Vrieslant inhoudende sekere peynen . . . *The Hague, A. Hendricksz.*, 1597. MPM.
H6

280* Danfrie, P. Déclaration de l'usage du graphometre, inventé nouvellement et mis en lumière par P. Danfrie. *Paris, P. Danfrie*, 1597. BN;
Bodl.   B4, 5

281* Habert, P. Le Miroir de vertu et chemin de bien vivre. *Paris, C.
Micard*, 1597. BM.   B1, 2

282 Vivre, G. de. Lettres missives familieres. *Rotterdam, J. van Waesberghe*, 1597. BB i, XXV, V 17. Ghent.   D1

283 Cordier, M. Les Colloques en latin et en françois. *Geneva, J.*   1598
Messery for Widow J. Durant, 1598. Geneva.   A1

284 La Case, I. de. Le Galatée [transl. by J. du Peyrat. *Geneva*], *J. de
Tournes*, 1598. Cartier 701. BM; MPM.   A2, 6, 8

285* Form of recognizance by victuallers. [*London, c.* 1599]. London, PRO,   1599
Class E180.   H2

286 Les Heures de Nostre Dame, latin-françois. *Metz, A. Faber*, 1599.
BN.   A2

287 Specimens of types sent by Guillaume II Le Bé to Jan Moretus. [*Paris,
c.* 1599] MPM, Arch. 153, fol. 2oh.   B1, 2

288 Cataneo, G. Le Capitaine. *Geneva, J. de Tournes*, 1600. Cartier 708.   1600
BM; Geneva.   A2, 6

289 [Lodewijcksz., W.] Le Second livre, iournal ou comptoir, contenant le   1601
vray discours . . . du voyage faict par huit navires d'Amsterdam . . .
l'an 1598. *Amsterdam, Corn. Nicolas for B. Dacivelle, Calais*, 1601. The
Hague.   H6

290* Jacquemot, J. Variorum poematum liber. [*Geneva*,] *J. de Tournes*,
1601. Cartier 711. BM; Geneva.   A2, 5, 6

291 Verhael . . . tegenwoirdighen staet van Nederlant. *Louvain, J. Maes*,
1601. MPM.   A2+E2

292* Derde vernieuwinge van de keuren . . . der stadt Leyden. *Leyden*,   1602
Raedthuys, 1602. Amsterdam, Coll. Hertzberger.   A4, 5, 6

293* Hout, J. van. Der stadt Leyden dienst-bouc. *Leyden, Raedthuys* [1602].
Amsterdam.   A4, 5, 6, D1

294 Het leven . . . van . . . S. Elena. *Louvain, J. Maes*, 1602. MPM. A2+E2

295 Jacobi, H. Den cleyne herbarius. *Amsterdam, H. Barentsz.*, 1603.   1603
Waller 858. The Hague.   D1

296 Nieuwe gheestelijcke refereynen. *Antwerp, G. Janssens*, 1603. MPM.
A2+E2

296a Spoelberch, W. Corte verclaringe van de principaelste mysterien . . .
der Missen. *Antwerp, G. Janssens,* 1603. Antwerp, Ruusbroec,
3114C2.   D1

297* Porquin, L. Den vvtersten vville van Lovvys Porquin. *Antwerp, J.
Trognesius,* 1603. Van Heurck 118, No. 149. MPM.   A2+E2

298 Copye van eenen brief geschreven van meester T. M. *Leyden, J.
Theunisz.* [*c.* 1603]. *Het Boek* 28 (1944–46), p. 16.   C2

299* Jossier, D. Poésie de David Jossier natif de Vitry-le François. [*Geneva,*   1604
J. de Tournes] 1604. Rothschild v, 3281. BN.   A1, 6.

300* James I, king of England. Form of letter demanding a forced loan,
31 July 1604. [*London, R. Barker,* 1604] STC 8356. Oxford, U.P. H2

301* James I, king of England. Form of letter recommending a collection
for the benefit of John Stow. [*London, R. Barker,* 1604] BM. MS. Harl.
367 (8).   H2

302 Coster, F. Verantwoorde . . . veur het tweede deel sijns schildts der   1605
catholijcken. *Antwerp, G. Janssens,* 1605. MPM.   A2+E2

303* [Aerts, H.] Den spiegel der jonkheyd. *Antwerp, G. Trognesius,* 1605.
MPM.   A2+E2

304* Guevara, A. de. Mespris de la cour. [*Geneva,*] *I. de Tournes,* 1605.
Cartier 720. BN; MPM.   A6, 8

305 Paradin, C. Alliances généalogiques des rois et princes de Gaule.   1606
Geneva, J. de Tournes, 1606. Geneva.   A6, 8

306* Den nieuwen, verbeterden lusthof. *Amsterdam,* [*D. P. Pers,*] 1607.   1607
The Hague, 1121 F 61(2); Leyden.   A5, 6

307 Const-thoonende iuweel. *Zwolle, Z. Heyns,* 1607–08. BB i, XIII, J37.
Bodl.; Ghent.   H6

308 [Heinsius, D.] Emblemata amatoria. *Amsterdam,* [s.n., 1608?]. The   1608
Hague, 1121 F 61 (1).   A6

309 Den nieuwen verbeterden lusthof. *Amsterdam, D. P. Pers,* 1608.
Amsterdam.   A5

310 Het wonderlijck schadtboek der historien . . . door P. Boaistuau, C. de
Tesserant ende R. Hoyer. *Antwerp, G. Janssens,* 1608. Antwerp;
Leyden.   D1

311 Cordier, M. Les Colloques. [*Geneva,*] *Widow of J. Durant,* 1608. See J.
Le Coultre, *Mathurin Cordier* (Neuchâtel, 1926), p. 404, fig. 34.   A1

312 Savonne, P. de. Brieve instruction pour tenir livres de raison. *Geneva,
J. de Tournes,* 1608. Cartier 749. BN.   A6

313 Houwaert, J. B. Pegasides pleyn. *Leyden, J. J. Paedts*, 1608. BB i, XII, H 88. Brussels; Ghent.   A4

314 [Lodewijcksz., W.] Le Second livre, iournal ou comptoir contenant   1609 le vray discours ... du voyage faict par huit navires d'Amsterdam ... l'an 1598. *Amsterdam, Corn. Nicolas*, 1609. Leyden.   H6

315 Peletier, J. L'Algebre. [*Geneva*,] *J. de Tournes*, 1609. Cartier 757. BN.   A2, 6

316 Vrancx, C. Vant alder rijckste. *Ghent, G. Manilius*, 1609. BB ii, XXVI, V 305. Ghent.   D1

317 Stevin, S. Le Trouve-port. *Leyden, C. Raphelengius*, 1609. The Hague.   A6

318 C., G. Bref instruction pour tous estats. *Pont-à-Mousson, M. Bernard*, 1609. BM.   B1

319 Smijters, A. Arithmetica. *Rotterdam, J. van Waesberghe*, 1609. Leyden.   D1

320 Bombaste, Le Comte de. Le Trompette françois. [s.l., s.n., 1609] BN.   B1

321 Makeblijde, L. Cathechismus, dat is de christelicken leeringhe. *Antwerp*,   1610 *J. Trognesius*, 1610. MPM.   A2+E2

322 Makeblijde, L. Den schat der christelicken leeringhe. *Antwerp, J. Trognesius*, 1610. MPM.   A4

323 Vrancx, C. Den sleutel des hemels. *Ghent, G. Manilius*, 1610. BB ii, XXVI, V 277. Ghent.   D1

324 La Civilité puerile, à laquelle auons adiousté la discipline et institution des enfans. *Lyons, H. Gazeau*, 1610. Paris, Coll. Scheler.   A2

325 Lessius, L. Beraedt wat gheloof ende religie men behoort te aenveerden.   1611 *Antwerp, Moretus*, 1611. Antwerp, Ruusbroec.   A5

326 [Scotland] The lawes and acts of Parliament ... *Edinburgh, T. Finlason*, 1611. STC 21878. Edinburgh, Univ. Lib.   A1

327 [Aysma, A.] Naeder waerschouwinghe over seeckere verantwoordingen D.D. Vorstii. *Leeuwarden, A. van den Rade*, 1611. The Hague, Pamphlet 1878.   H5

328* Houwaert, J. B. Pegasides pleyn. *Leyden, J. Paedts*, 1611. BB i, XII, H 16. Brussels.   A4

329* Lect, J. Pro Errico IV. [*Geneva*,] *J. de Tournes*, 1611. Cartier 764. Geneva.   A2

330* Houwaert, J. B. Den generalen loop der vverelt. *Amsterdam, B.*   1612 *Otsz. for G. Stam*, 1612. BB i, XII, H 27. Brussels.   A5

331 [Heinsius, D.] Emblemata amatoria. *Amsterdam, D. P. Pers,* 1612.
     The Hague.   A6

332* James I, king of England. Verklaringhe van der alderdoorluchtich-
     sten koning van groot Brittannien over de handelingen met de
     Staten Generaal van der vereenichte Nederlanden nopende het feyt van
     Conradus Vorstius. *Amsterdam,* s.n., 1612. BM.   C1

333 Verclaringhe der kercken-dienaers tot Leeuwarden over D. Vorstii
     volcomener antwoordt. *Leeuwarden, A. vanden Rade,* 1612. BM. C1

334* [Visscher, R.] t'Loff vande mutse ende van een blaeuwe scheen.
     Leyden, J. Paedts, 1612. Antwerp.   A6

335* James I, king of England. Form of letter demanding a forced loan,
     2.1.1612. [*London,* s.n., 1612]. STC 8460. Oxford, U.P.   H2

336* James I, king of England. Form of letter demanding a forced loan for
     military purposes in Ireland, April, 1612. [s.l., s.n.] STC 9236. Bodl.,
     MS. Rawl. D 366, fol. 14.   H2

337* Smijters, A. Schrijf kunst boeck. *Amsterdam, N. Biestkens,* 1613. 1613
     Amsterdam.   D1

338 Guevara, A. de. Misprijsinghe ende miserie des hofs. *Delft, A. Gerrits,*
     1613. The Hague.   A4

339 Cordier, M. Les Colloques...en latin et en francois. [*Geneva,*]
     Widow of J. Durant, 1613. Geneva.   A1

340 [Lescarbot, M.] Les Bains de Fewer...en Suisse. [*Geneva,*] *J. de
     Tournes,* 1613. Rothschild iv, 2950. BN.   A1, 2, 6

341* A briefe of the Bill concerning printers. [*London, for the Co. of
     Stationers, c.* 1613]. BM, Ames 1, p. 58.   H2

342 [Spiegel, H. L.?] Twe-spraack vande Nederduitsche letterkunst. 1614
     Amsterdam, H. Barentsz., 1614. BB i, XXIV, T. 17. Ghent.   D1

343* Houwa[e]rt, J. B. Politijcke onderwijsinghe. *Leeuwarden, A. vanden
     Rade,* 1614. Waller 839. BM; The Hague.   H5

344* Houwaert, J. B. De vier wterste. *Leeuwarden, A. vanden Rade, for
     B. Arents,* 1614. BB i, XII, H 23. BM; Brussels.   H5

345 Materi-boecxken oft voorschriften...om wel te leeren lesen. *Utrecht,
     H. Hendricksz. van Borculo,* 1614. Utrecht, Gemeentearchief. A4

346* Heyns, Z. Emblemata: volsinnighe uytbeelsels. *Arnhem, J. Janszen,* 1615
     1615. Ghent.   H6

347* Form of lease by Hugh Myddelton of water-supply from the New 1616
     River. [*London,* s.n.] 1616. Oxford, U.P.   H7

348 Lusthof der ghebeden. *Antwerp, G. Janssens,* [*c.* 1618]. Antwerp. A4 1618

349* Rodenburgh, T. Eglentiers poëtens borst-weringh. *Amsterdam, P.*   1619
     van Ravesteyn for J. E. Cloppenburgh. 1619. BM.   A6

350 Cécier, J.-D., sieur de Colony. La Voye de la vie éternelle. [*Geneva,*]
     F. Le Fevr[e], 1619. Geneva.   A1, 2, 6

351 Boaistuau, P. Le Theatre du monde. *Geneva, J. de Tournes,* 1619.
     Geneva.   A2, 6, 8

352 Den nieuwen verbeterden lusthof. *Amsterdam, D. P. Pers,* 1620. 1620
     The Hague.   A5, 6

353 Vondel, J. van. De heerlijckheyd van Salomon. *Amsterdam, D. P.*
     Pers, 1620. Amsterdam.   A6

354 Vondel, J. van. Jerusalem verwoest. *Amsterdam, D. P. Pers,* 1620.
     Amsterdam.   A6

355 [Furmerius, B.] Recht ghebruyck ende misbruyck van tydlicke have
     [transl. by D. V. Coornhert]. *Amsterdam, P.A. van Ravesteyn for D.P.*
     Pers, 1620. BB i, VI, C 59. BM; Ghent.   A6

356 Vondel, J. van. De helden godes des ouwden verbonds. *Amsterdam,*
     P. A. van Ravesteyn for D. P. Pers, 1620. Amsterdam.   A6

357* Heyns, Z. W. S. Heere van Bartas wercken. *Amsterdam, P. A. van*   1621
     Ravesteyn for Z. Heyns, Zwolle, 1621. BB i, XII, H 66. Brussels. A6

358 Starter, J. J. Friesche lust-hof. *Amsterdam, P. A. van Ravesteyn,* 1621.
     Antwerp.   A6

359 Evangelien ende epistelen. *Antwerp, J. Mesens,* 1621. Oosterhout, St.
     Paulus Abbey.   D1

360* Bredero, G. A. Groot liedboeck. *Amsterdam, C. L. vander Plasse,* 1622. 1622
     Antwerp, Coll. Dirkx.   A6

361 V[ondel], J. van. De vernieuwde gulden winckel der kunstlievende
     Nederlanders. *Amsterdam, P. A. van Ravesteyn for D. P. Pers,*
     1622. Antwerp.   A6

362 Coutereels, J. Den vasten stijl van boeckhouden. *Middelburgh, S.* 1623
     Moulert, 1623. Leyden.   A6, D1

363* Verbal de l'invention du vray charbon de terre par toute la France. [s.l., 1626
     s.n.,] 1626. BN, Rés. S. 1110.   B4, 5

364 Dafforne, R. Grammatica ofte leez-leerlings steunsel. *Amsterdam,* 1627
     J. E. Kloppenburgh, 1627. Leyden.   D1

365 Zachmoorter, M. Bruydegoms beddeken. *Antwerp, G. van Wols-*   1628
     schaten, 1628. Antwerp.   A2

366 Ampzing, S. Beschrijvinghe en lof der stad Haerlem in Holland.
     Haarlem, A. Rooman, 1628. Amsterdam.   A6

367   Placcaet ende ordonnantie . . . van Frederik Hendrik . . . op de
      groote ongeregeltheden . . . in't iaghen. *The Hague, Widow of Hille-*
      brandt Iacobsz. van Wouw, 1628. The Hague.   A5, 6

368   Loris, [D.] Le Thresor des parterres de l'univers. *Geneva, E. Gamonet,*   1629
      1629. Paris, Coll. Scheler.   A6

369   Den bloemhof van de Nederlantsche ieught . . . *Amsterdam, D. P.*   1630
      Pers, 1630. The Hague.   A6

370   Resolutie bij de heeren raeden en vroedschappen der stadt Haerlem . . .
      nopende 't stuck vanden Treves. *Haarlem, A. Rooman,* 1630. Antwerp.
                                                                       A6

371   Coutereels, J. Constige interest-rekeninghen. *Flushing, S. Claeys Ver-*   1631
      sterre, 1631. Leyden.   D1

372* Bredero, G. A. Alle de wercken. *Amsterdam, C. L. van der Plasse,*   1632
      1632–38. Waller 328. The Hague.   A5

373   Heusden, R. van. Livre de comptes pour apprendre à jetter. *Antwerp,*   1635
      C. J. Trognesius, 1635. BB iii, fasc. 220, No. H 260. Brussels.   E2a

374   Coote, E. The English scolemaister. *London, T. P[urfoot],* 1636. STC   1636
      5715. BM.   H7

375   [Aerts, H.] Den spiegel der jonckheyd. *Antwerp, G. Lesteens* [c. 1640].   1640
      MPM.   D1

376* Barnard, J. Book of selected church musick. *London, E. Griffin,* 1641. 1641
      Wing 853. BM.   H8

377   Tengnagel, M. G. Het leven van Konstance. *Amsterdam, N. van*   1643
      Ravesteyn, 1643. Antwerp.   A4

378   Bijns, A. Konstige refereynen. *Antwerp, Verdussen,* 1646. Antwerp,   1646
      Coll. Dirckx.   E2a

379   Heusden, R. van. Reken-boecksken om te leerē leggē eñ rekenen met   1647
      penningē. *Antwerp, M. Verhulst,* s.d. [c. 1647]. BB iii, H 264. Brussels.
                                                                       A2+E2

380   Manierlijcke zeden betoonde bij vraeghen ende antwoorden. *Antwerp,*
      M. Verhulst, 1647. Leyden.   A2+E2

381   [Coornhert, D. V.] Ruygh-bewerp vande redenkaveling. *Amsterdam,*
      G. Willemsz. [1649]. The Hague.   A6

382   Kort begrip leerende recht Duidts spreken. *Amsterdam, G. Willemsz.,*
      1649. BB i, II, B 43. Brussels.   A6

383* La Civilité puerile et honneste pour l'instruction des enfants. *Troyes,*   1649
      N. Oudot, 1649. BN.   A2

384   Bie, C. de. Den groeiyenden Lierschen blomhof. *Antwerp, J. Mesens,*   1650
      1650. Antwerp.   C2

385 Linden, J. van der. Reyse nae . . . Jerusalem. *Antwerp, G. Verhulst,*
     1650. Ghent.   A2+E2

386 Dale, J. vanden. De vre van der doot. *Delft, Widow of A. Havelaers,*   1652
     1652. BB i, VIII, D 8. The Hague.   A4+D1

386a Proeven der letteren . . . Wed. Broer Jansz. *Amsterdam, Widow of*   1653
     Broer Janszoon, 1653. Leyden, 1207A1.   A4, D1, H9

387* Porquin, L. Den vvtersten vville. *Leeuwarden, G. Sybes,* 1653.
     Brussels.   A4

388* Porquin, L. Den vvtersten vville. *Antwerp, G. Verhulst,* 1655. Ghent.   1655
                                                           A2+E2

389* De schoone historie van den vroomen en godvrugtigen jongeling   1658
     Joseph. *Bruges, N. Breygel,* 1658. Ghent.   E2a

390* Form of bond for performance of covenants. [*London,* s.n., 1660]   1660
     Oxford, U.P.   H7

391* Form of licence by the Regius Professor of Divinity and Vice-
     Chancellor of the University of Oxford to eat meat in lent. [s.l., s.n.,]
     [1660]. Bodl., G. A. Oxon b 19.   H7

392* Hondert schoone exempelen tot 't bewys der deughden. *Antwerp, L.*   1661
     van Diest, 1661. Van Heurck 12, No. 14. Brussels.   E2a

393 [Arcerius, J.] Een nuttelijk voor-schrift-boexken. *Franeker, J.*   1662
     Arcerius, 1662. Amsterdam.   D1

394 Coote, E. The English school-master. *London, W. Leybourn for the*
     Co. of Stationers, 1662. Wing 6069. BM.   H7

395 Coote, E. The English school-master. *London, W. Leybourn for the*   1665
     Co. of Stationers., 1665. Wing 6071. BM.   H7

396 Coote, E. The English school-master. *London, E. Tyler for the Co.*   1669
     of Stationers, 1669. Wing 6072. Bodl.   H7

397 Proverbia ofte spreuken . . . Salomonis. *Amsterdam, C. Lootsman,*   1672
     [p. 1672]. Amsterdam.   E3

398 Coote, E. The English school-master. *London, A. Maxwell for the Co.*   1673
     of Stationers, 1673. Wing 6074. BM.   H7

399 [Aerts, H.] Den spieghel der ionckheydt. *Antwerp, J. Mesens,* 1675.   1675
     Van Heurck 96, No. 123.   E3

400 Heusden, R. van. Reken-boecksken. *Antwerp, J. Mesens,* 1676.   1676
     Antwerp.   A2+E2, E3

401 [Jacobi, H.] Ghemeyne send-brieven. *Antwerp, J. Mesens,* 1676.
     Antwerp.   A2+E2

402   Honderd schoone exempelen. *Antwerp, G. van Heylen,* 1677. Antwerp.   1677
       D1

403   [Jacobi, H.] Gemeyne zend-brieven, zeer profytelyk voor d'ouders,
       meesters &c. *Antwerp, G. van Heylen,* 1677. Antwerp.   D1

404   Porquin, L. Den uytersten wille. *Amsterdam, J. Bouman,* 1680.   1680
       BM.   D1

405 * Form of certificate of the grant of letters of administration on intestacy.
       [*London,* s.n., 1680] Oxford, U.P.   H7

406 * Form of certificate of the grant of probate. [*London,* s.n., 1680] Oxford,
       U.P.   H7

407   [Aerts, H.] Den spiegel der jonkheyd. *Antwerp, G. van Heylen,* 1683.   1683
       Ghent.   D1

408   [Aerts, H.] Den spiegel der jonkheyd. *Antwerp, J. Jacops,* 1683.
       Antwerp.   E1

409   De historie van den ouden Tobias. *Antwerp, J. Jacops,* 1683. MPM.
       E2

410   Hondert schoone exempelen. *Antwerp, Widow of J. Willemsens,* 1683.
       Antwerp.   E1

411   Porquin, L. Den uyttersten wille. *Utrecht, J. van Poolsum,* 1687.   1687
       BM.   A6, D1

412   Porquin, L. Den vvtersten vville. *Amsterdam, J. Bouman,* 1690.   1690
       Leyden.   D1

413 * Form of certificate of the grant of letters of administration on intestacy.
       [*London,* s.n., 1690] Oxford, U.P.   H7

414   Proef van letteren . . . Weduwe van Dirk Voskens en Zonen. *Amster-*   1691
       dam, Widow of D. Voskens [p. 1691]. MPM, Fol. Var. ii, fol. 105.
       D1, H1

415   Linden, J. van der. Heerelycke ende geluckige reyse . . . Jerusalem.   1692
       Antwerp, G. van Gaesbeeck [p. 1692]. Brussels.   E3

416   [Aerts, H.] Den spiegel der jonckheydt. *Antwerp, J. van Gaesbeeck,*
       [p. 1692]. Antwerp, Ruusbroec.   E3

417   Proeven van veelerhande . . . letteren. *Hoorn, P. Boeyesz.,* 1692.
       Leyden.   D1, H9

418   Porquin, L. Den uyterste wille. *Dordrecht, S. Onder de Linde,* 1693.   1693
       Amsterdam.   D1

419   Jacobi, H. Gemeene send-brieven voor d'ouders. *The Hague, P. van*   1695
       Santen, [p. 1695]. Waller 860. The Hague.   D1

420   Vos, J. B. de. Reken-boecxken. *Antwerp, J. Gymnicus* [c. 1696].   1696
       MPM.   E3

421 [Type-specimen of Melchior van Wolsschaten, *Antwerp*, p. 1701?].   1701
     MPM, Fol. Var. i, fol. 112 *bis*.   E1, 2, 3

422 Hakvoord, B. Gemene zend-brieven. *Schiedam, N. Muys* [p. 1705].   1705
     Waller 659. The Hague.   D1

423 [Hakvoord, B.] Gemeyne zend-brieven. *Zwolle, E. B. Hakvoord*, 1712.   1712
     Antwerp.   A4

424 De proverbia ofte spreuken ... Salomons. *Deventer, E. de Vries*,   1715
     1715. Amsterdam.   D1

425 De fonteyne der eeren: La Fontaine d'honneur. *Brussels, Widow of*   1716
     G. Stryckwant, 1716. Haarlem, Enschedé.   E3

426 Proef van letteren die te bekomen zyn by Isaac vander Putte. *Amster-*   1717
     dam, I. vander Putte [p. 1717]. MPM, Fol. Var, ii, fol. 99.   A4

427 Jacobi, H. Ghemeyne sendbrieven. *Antwerp, J. Gymnicus*, 1717.
     Brussels.   E3

428 De kleyne christelijke academie. *Antwerp, H. Verdussen* [c. 1717?].
     Ghent, Bl.5902.   D1, E2a

429 [Linden, J. van der.] Heerlycke ende gheluckighe reyse ... nae
     Jerusalem. *Antwerp, Widow of J. Woons*, 1717. Van Heurck 82,
     No. 103. Brussels.   E3

430 [Aerts, H.] Den spiegel der jonkheyd. *Antwerp, M. Verdussen* [p. 1720].   1720
     Antwerp.   E2a

431 De ghestichtige historie van den ouden ende jongen Tobias. *Antwerp*,
     M. Verdussen [p. 1720]. Van Heurck, 53, No. 62. Brussels.   D1, E2a

432 De historie vanden ouden Tobias. *Antwerp, M. Verdussen* [p. 1720].
     Antwerp.   E2a

433 De kleyne christelycke academie. *Antwerp, M. Verdussen* [p. 1720].
     Antwerp, Ruusbroec.   E3

434 [Thienen, F. van.] De historie van den conincklijcken propheet David.
     Antwerp, M. Verdussen [p. 1720]. Van Heurck 21, No. 25. MPM.   E3

435 [Jacobi, H.] Gemeyne zend-brieven. *Louvain, F. Vande Velde* [c. 1720].
     Ghent.   E2a

436 Jacobi, H. Ghemeyne sendbrieven. *Antwerp, J. Gymnicus*, 1721.   1721
     Brussels.   E3

437 Pistorius, J. [Typefounder's specimen] *Basle*, 1721. See A. Bruckner,
     Schweizer Stempelschneider und Schriftgiesser (Basle, 1943), p. 60.   A1

438 De historie van den ouden ende jongen Tobias. *Antwerp, J. F. van*   1722
     Soest [p. 1722]. Ghent.   E3

439 Jacobi, H. Gemeyne sent-brieven voor ouders. *Antwerp, J. F. van*
     Soest [p. 1722]. Waller 859. The Hague.   E2a

440 De kleyne christelycke academie. *Antwerp, J. F. van Soest* [p. 1722].
Van Heurck, 7, No. 5. Brussels. E2a

441 Hondert schoone exempelen tot aanwysinghe der deughden. *Antwerp,* 1723
M. Verdussen, 1723. Van Heurck 14, No. 15. Brussels; Ghent. E3

442 Linden, J. van der. Het weder-keeren . . . reyse . . . nae Jerusalem. 1724
Antwerp, J. Gymnicus, 1724. MPM. E3

443 Hakvoord, B. Gemene zend-brieven. *Sneek, A. Olingius* [c. 1724].
Waller 660. The Hague. A4

444 [Aerts, H.] Den spiegel der jonkheyd. *Antwerp, Widow of J. Gymnicus* 1728
[p. 1728]. Antwerp. E3

445 Proeve van . . . capitalen . . . die gegoten worden by Hendrik Bruyn 1729
en comp. . . . in de Stilsteeg tot Amsterdam. *Amsterdam, H. Bruyn*
[p. 1729]. BN, Rés. Atlas Q21, fol. 113, Haarlem, Enschedé. D1, H9

446 Hakvoord, B. Gemeene zendbrieven. *Amsterdam, I. vander Putte,* 1735
1735. Amsterdam. A2 + A4

447* La Civilité françoise pour l'instruction de la jeunesse. *Liège, J. F.*
Bassompierre [p. 1735]. BM. E2a

448 Hondert schoone exempelen. *Antwerp, J. F. van Soest,* 1736. Antwerp. 1736
E3

449 [Aerts, H.] Den spiegel der jonkheyd. *Ghent, J. Meyer* [p. 1737].
Ghent. E2a

450 Honderd schoone exempelen. *Ghent, J. Meyer* [p. 1737]. Ghent; 1737
Brussels. E2a

451 De kleine christelyke academie. *Ghent, J. Meyer* [c. 1737]. Ghent,
G 2283. E2a

452 [Linden, J. van der]. Eerlyke ende gelukkige reyse nae . . . Jerusalem.
Ghent, J. Meyer [p. 1737]. Ghent. E2a

453 De schoone historie van den vromen en godvruchtigen jongeling
Joseph. *Ghent, J. Meyer* [p. 1737]. Van Heurck 23, No. 28. Brussels;
Ghent. E2a

454 [Thienen, F. van.] De historie van den koninklyken propheet David.
Ghent, J. Meyer [p. 1737]. Van Heurck 23, No. 28. Brussels; Ghent.
E2a

455 Conduite pour la bienséance civile. *Lyons,* [A.?] *Périsse* [p. 1737].
Haarlem, Enschedé. A4

456 La Civilité honnête. *Troyes, Widow Garnier* [p. 1738]. BN. B1 1738

457 Materie ofte spelde-boecxken. *Utrecht, H. J. Bosch,* 1738. Waller
1171. The Hague. A4, H9

458 [Linden, J. van der.] Heerlyke ende geluckige reyse nae . . . Jerusalem. 1740
Antwerp, *Widow of H. Thieullier*, 1740. MPM. E3

459 Epreuves générales des caractères qui se trouvent chez Claude Lamesle. 1742
Paris, C. Lamesle, 1742. BN; London, St. Bride. B1, 2

460 [Linden, J. van der.] Heerelycke ende geluckige reyse nae . . . Jeru- 1744
salem. *Brussels, Widow of G. Jacobs*, 1744. Van Heurck 85, No. 113.
Brussels. E3

461 Jacobi, H. Gemeyne send-brieven. *Antwerp, Widow of H. Verdussen* 1745
[*c.* 1745]. Van Heurck 124, No. 152. Antwerp; Brussels; MPM,
A3535. E2a

462 Linden, J. van der. Heerlycke ende geluckige reyse naer . . . Jerusalem.
Antwerp, Widow of H. Verdussen [*c.* 1745]. Antwerp; Brussels; MPM,
A 3014. E2a

463 De proverbia ofte spreuken . . . Salomonis. *Deventer, E. de Vries*,
1745. Amsterdam. D1

464 Linden, J. van der. Heerlycke ende geluckige reyze nae . . . Jerusalem. 1746
Antwerp, Widow of H. Thieullier & H. Colpijn [*p.* 1746]. Ghent. E3

465 La Civilité honnête. *Caen, P. Chalopin* [*p.* 1746]. BM. B1

466 Proef van letteren die te bekomen zyn by Hendrik vander Putte. 1748
Amsterdam, H. vander Putte [*p.* 1748]. BM; MPM, Fol. Var. ii, fol. 96.
A4

467 Jacobi, H. Gemeene send-brieven voor d'ouders. *The Hague, C. van* 1751
Zanten, 1751. Waller 861. The Hague. D1

468 Jacobi, H. Gemeyne zend-brieven voor ouders. *Antwerp, H. Bincken* 1753
[*p.* 1753]. Waller 862. Brussels; Ghent; The Hague. E3

469 De klyne christelyke academie. *Antwerp, H. Bincken* [*p.* 1753]. Brussels; Ghent; MPM, R 12.15. E3

470 [Thienen, F. van.] De historie van den koninglyken propheet David.
Antwerp, H. Bincken [*p.* 1753]. Antwerp; Ghent; MPM, A 3015. E3

471 La Civilité Puerile et honneste pour l'instruction des enfans . . . 1757
dressée par un missionaire. *Paris, C. Hérissant*, 1757. BM. B1

472 Proef van letteren. *Amsterdam, Clerk, Voskens* [*c.* 1760]. MPM, Fol. 1760
Var. ii, fol. 108. D1, H1

473 Linden, J. van der. Heerlyke ende gelukkige reyze naer . . . Jerusalem.
Antwerp, J. Verdussen [*p.* 1760]. Antwerp. E3

474 [Thienen, F. van.] De historie van den conincklycken profeet David.
Antwerp, J. Verdussen [*c.* 1760]. Antwerp; Brussels. E3

475 Heures nouvelles dédiées à Madame Royale. *Brussels, J. J. Boucherie*
[1760]. Brussels. E2

476 Epreuves des caractères de la fonderie de Gando père et fils. *Paris*, [*Gando*], 1760. London, St. Bride. B1, B2

477 Cramer, B. De Geldersche trap der jeugd. *Amsterdam, A. Meijer* 1761 [p. 1761]. Waller 432. The Hague. C1, A4

478 [Aerts, H.] Den spiegel der jonkheyd. *Antwerp, H. Verdussen* [p. 1761]. Antwerp. E2

479 [Linden, J. van der.] Heerlyke en gelukkige reys naer . . Jerusalem. *Antwerp, H. Verdussen* [p. 1761]. Van Heurck 84, No. 107. Brussels. E2a

480 Woorden-schat ofte letter-konste. *Ghent, Widow of M. de Goesin* [p. 1761]. Waller 1893. The Hague. E3

481 De schoone historie van den vroomen en godvrugtigen jongeling 1764 Joseph. *Bruges, J. B. Macqué*, 1764. Ghent. A4

482 Fournier, [S.-P.] le jeune. Manuel typographique. *Paris*, [*S.-P. Fournier*], 1764–66. BM; BN; Bodl.; London, St. Bride; MPM. A2+B1

483 A specimen [of types]. *London, T. Cottrell* [*c.* 1765]. Berry & John- 1765 son, p. 34. Stockholm, Kon. Bibl., Sohmian Coll. F1

484 [Aerts, H.] Den spiegel der jonkheyd. *Antwerp, J. P. Willemsens* 1766 [*c.* 1766]. Ghent. E3

485 De historie van den ouden Tobias. *Antwerp, J. P. Willemsens* [*c.* 1766]. MPM, A 2093. E3

486 [Thienen, F. van.] De historie van den koninglyken propheet David. *Bruges, P. Roose*, 1766. Antwerp. A4

487 A specimen of printing types. *London, T. Cottrell* [*c.* 1766]. Berry & Johnson, p. 35. London, St. Bride. F1

488 Epreuve de lettres, fleurons, signes . . . *Amsterdam, Ploos van Amstel* 1767 [1767]. BM; MPM. A2, 4

489 Proef van letteren, bloemen, tekenen . . . *Amsterdam, Ploos van Amstel*, 1767. BM; MPM. A2, 4

490 Honderd schoone exempelen. *Antwerp, P. J. Rymers* [p. 1767]. Antwerp. E3

491* Jacobi, H. Gemeyne zend-brieven. *Antwerp, P. J. Rymers* [p. 1767]. BM; Ghent. E3

492 [Linden, J. van der.] Eerlyke ende gelukkige reyze nae . . . Jerusalem. *Antwerp, P. J. Rymers* [p. 1767]. Ghent. E3

493 [Aerts, H.] Den spiegel der jonkheyd. *Antwerp, F. I. Vinck* [p. 1768]. 1768 Antwerp; Brussels; Ghent. E3

494   [Jacobi, H.] Gemeyne zend-brieven. *Antwerp, F. I. Vinck* [p. 1768].
       Antwerp; Brussels; Ghent; MPM.   E3

495   De historie van den ouden Tobias. *Antwerp, F. I. Vinck* [p. 1768].
       Antwerp; MPM.   E3

496   Honderd schoone exempelen tot aenwysinge der deugden. *Antwerp,*
       F. I. Vinck [p. 1768]. Van Heurck 14, No. 16. Brussels; MPM, A
       2767.   E3

497   De klyne christelyke academie. *Antwerp, F. I. Vinck* [p. 1768].
       Antwerp; MPM, A 2100.   E3

498   [Thienen, F. van.] De historie van den koniglyken propheet David.
       Antwerp, F. I. Vinck [p. 1768]. Van Heurck 22, No. 27; Waller 768.
       Amsterdam; Brussels; MPM; The Hague.   E3

499   Epreuve des caractères qui se gravent et fondent dans la nouvelle fon-
       derie de Jacques François Rosart. *Brussels* [*J.-F. Rosart*], 1768.
       London, St. Bride; MPM.   B1

500   Historie van den jongeling Joseph. *Ghent, J. Begyn* [p. 1768]. Waller
       757. Antwerp; Ghent; The Hague.   G1

501   Honderd schoone exempelen tot bewys der deugden. *Ghent. J. Begyn*
       [p. 1768]. Van Heurck 15, No. 19. Brussels; Ghent.   G1

502   De kleyne christelyke academie. *Ghent, J. Begyn* [p. 1768]. Antwerp,
       Ruusbroec; Brussels; Ghent.   G1

503   [Linden, J. van der.] Heerlyke ende gelukkige reyze nae ... Jeruza-
       lem. *Ghent, J. Begyn* [p. 1768]. Van Heurck 86, No. 117. Antwerp;
       Brussels; Ghent.   G1

504   [Linden, J. van der.] Heerlyke ende gelukkige reyze nae ... Jerusalem.
       Ghent, J. Begyn [p. 1768]. Van Heurck 86, No. 115. Antwerp;
       Ghent.   E2a

505   [Linden, J. van der.] Het wederkeeren ... reyze ... nae Jerusalem.
       Ghent, J. Begyn [p. 1768]. Antwerp; Brussels; Ghent.   G1

506   Den nieuwen spiegel der jongheyd of gulden ABC. *Ghent, J. Begyn,*
       1768. Antwerp; Ghent.   G1

507   [Thienen, F. van.] De historie van den koninglyken propheet David.
       Ghent, J. Begyn [p. 1768]. Antwerp, Ruusbroec; Brussels; Ghent. G1

508   Proef van letteren. *Haarlem, J. Enschedé,* 1768. Haarlem, Enschedé;
       London, St. Bride.   A2+H5, H3

509   A specimen of printing types. *London, T. Cottrell* [c. 1768]. Berry &
       Johnson, pp. 35–6. Oxford, U.P.   F1

510   Gelliers, C. de. Trap der jeugd. *Amsterdam, Adam Meijer* [1769].   1769
       The Hague.   D1

511 [Aerts, H.] Den spiegel der jonkheyd. *Brussels, G. Pauwels* [p. 1769].
     Ghent.   E2a

512 De klyne christelyke academie. *Brussels, G. Pauwels* [p. 1769].
     Brussels.   E2a

513 Christelyke academie. *Malines, Van Velsen-van der Elst* [p. 1769].
     Antwerp, Ruusbroec.   G1

514 [Luckombe, P.] Concise history of printing. *London, W. Adlard &*   1770
     J. Browne, 1770. Berry & Johnson, p. 36. London, St. Bride.   F1

515 Linden, J. van der. Eerlyke ende gelukkige reyze nae . . . Jerusalem.   1771
     Ghent, Widow of J. Meyer [p. 1771]. Waller 1722. The Hague.   E2a

515a Proeve van . . . letteren . . . verzameld door Joannes Kannewet.
     Amsterdam, J. Kannewet & P. Schouten, 1771. Amsterdam, Bibl. der
     Vereniging ter Bevordering des Boekhandels.   H9

516 Luckombe, P. History and art of printing. *London, W. Adlard &*
     J. Brown, 1771. Berry & Johnson, p. 36. BM; Oxford, U.P.   F1

517 Den nieuwen spiegel der jongheyt. *Ypres, T. Walwein,* 1772. Antwerp,   1772
     Ruusbroec.   E2

518 Les Caractères et les vignettes du sieur Delacolonge. *Lyons, [L.] Dela-*   1773
     colonge, 1773. BN; London, St. Bride.   A2, 5, 6, 8

519 De proverbia ofte spreuken . . . Salomons. *Amsterdam, J. Kannewet,*   1774
     1774. Amsterdam.   A4+D1

520 La Salle, J.-B. de. Les Règles de la bienséance et de la civilité chrétienne.
     Rheims, P.-N.-A. Pierard, 1774. BN, R 40851.   B1

521 La Salle, J.-B. de. Les Règles de la bienséance et de la civilité chrétienne.
     Rheims, P.-N.-A. Pierard [c. 1774]. BN, R 40849.   B1

522 La Salle, J.-B. de. Les Règles de la bienséance et de la civilité chré-
     tienne. *Rheims, P.-N.-A. Pierard* [c. 1774]. BN, R 40847.   A2+B1

523 Linden, J. van der. Eerlyke ende gelukkige reyze . . . nae Jeruzalem.   1775
     Ghent, P. F. Cocquyt [p. 1775]. Ghent.   E2a

524 Civilité honnête pour l'instruction des enfants. *Paris, C. F. Berton,*
     1775. BN.   B1

525 [Linden, J. van der.] Heerlye ende gelukkige reyze nae . . . Jerusalem.   1776
     Antwerp, J. P. De Cort, 1776. MPM.   E3

526 Epreuves [Type specimen]. *J. L. de Boubers, Brussels,* 1777. Haarlem,   1777
     Enschedé; London, St. Bride.   G1

527 [Aerts, H.] Den spiegel der jonkheyd. *Brussels, N. Jacobs,* 1777.
     Ghent.   E3

528 Epreuve des caractères ... de la Veuve Decellier, successeur de J. F. 1779
Rosart. *Brussels, Widow Decellier*, 1779. MPM.   B1

529 Christelyke academie. *Lier, J. H. Le Tellier* [p. 1779]. Brussels, VI
1575 A.   E3

530 [Linden, J. van der.] Wederkomste ... reyze ... nae Jerusalem. 1780
Antwerp, J. E. Parijs [p. 1780]. MPM.   E2a

531 Nieuwe gemeyne zendbrieven. *Bruges, M. de Sloovere* [c. 1780]. Ghent,
G 2802/2.   E2a

532 De schoone historie van den vroomen en godvrugtigen jongeling
Joseph. *Bruges, M. de Sloovere* [c. 1780]. Ghent.   E2a

533 Honderd schoone exempelen. *Lier, J. H. Le Tellier* [c. 1780].
Antwerp, Ruusbroec; Brussels.   E3

534 [Paterson, S.] A catalogue and specimen of sundry printing materials 1781
[of E. Rowe Mores. ... *London*, s.n., 1781]. London, St. Bride. F1

535 [Paterson, S.] A catalogue and specimen of the printing-type foundery 1782
of ... Mr. John James. [*London*, s.n., 1782]. Berry & Johnson, p. 4.
New York, Grolier Club; Providence, R.I.   H2

536 La Salle, J.-B. de. Les Règles de la bienséance et de la civilité chrétienne.
Rheims, P.-N.-A. Pierard, 1782. BN.   B1

537 La Civilité puerile et honneste pour l'instruction des enfans ... 1785
dressée par un missionnaire. *Paris, chez Onfroy*, 1785. BM.   B1

538 De kleyne christelyke academie. *Ypres, S. Ramoen*, 1786. Antwerp, 1786
Ruusbroec.   E2

539 Honderd schoone exempelen tot bewys der deugden. *Ghent, B.* 1787
Poelman [p. 1787]. Antwerp, Ruusbroec; Ghent; Brussels.   E2a

540 De kleyne christelyke academie. *Ghent, B. Poelman* [p. 1787].
Antwerp; Antwerp, Ruusbroec; Brussels; The Hague.   E2a

541 [Linden, J. van der.] Eerlyke ende gelukkige reyze nae ... Jerusalem.
Ghent, B. Poelman [p. 1787]. Van Heurck 81, No. 119; Waller 1723.
Brussels; The Hague.   E2a

542 [Linden, J. van der.] Eerlyke ende gelukkige reyze ... nae Jerusalem,
2e. deel: Het wederkeren. *Ghent, B. Poelman* [p. 1787]. Antwerp;
Ghent.   E2a

543 De schoone historie van den vromen en godvruchtigen jongeling
Joseph. *Ghent, B. Poelman* [p. 1787]. Antwerp, Ruusbroec; Brussels;
Ghent.   E2a

544 [Thienen, F. van.] De historie van den koninglyken propheet David.
Ghent, B. Poelman [p. 1787]. Antwerp, Ruusbroec; Brussels.   E2a

544a De kleene christelyke academie. *Bruges, M. J. Lacroix* [c. 1788]. 1788
Van Heurck 9, No. 11. Brussels, III 92875 A.   G1

545 Den nieuwen spiegel der jongheyd of gulden ABC. *Bruges, C. De Moor*, 1788. Antwerp, Ruusbroec. 2095 D 62.   B1

546 Hakvoord, B. Gemeene zend-brieven. *Deventer, J. de Lange*, 1788. Waller 662. The Hague.   D1

547 Jacobi, H. Gemeyne send-brieven voor ouders. *Antwerp, J. N. Vinck* 1789 [p. 1789]. Waller 683. Brussels; Ghent; MPM; The Hague.   E3

548 Honderd schoone exempelen. *Antwerp, J. N. Vinck* [p. 1789]. Brussels; Ghent; MPM.   E3

549 [Linden, J. van der.] Eerlyke ende gelukkige reyse nae . . . Jerusalem. *Antwerp, J. N. Vinck* [p. 1789]. Van Heurck 85, No. 110. MPM, A 3506.   E3

550 Hakvoord, B. Gemeene zendbrieven. *Deventer, J. de Lange*, 1790. 1790 Brussels.   D1

551 La Civilité honneste. *Rouen, P. Seyer & Behourt* [p. 1790]. Haarlem, Enschedé.   B1

552 Hakvoord, B. Gemeene zend-brieven. *Leyden, D. du Mortier & Zn.*, 1792 1792. Waller 663. The Hague.   D1

553 Hakvoord, B. Algemene zend-brieven. *Amsterdam,* [*J. Bouwer &* 1793 *J. Ratelband*] 1793. Amsterdam.   D1

554 Hakvoord, B. Gemene zend-brieven. *Amsterdam, J. Ratelband & J. Bouwer* [*c.* 1793]. Waller 664. The Hague.   D1

555 De kleyne christelyke academie. *Antwerp, J. H. Heiliger* [p. 1793]. Antwerp; Brussels; MPM.   D1

555a Proeve van letteren . . . ter boekdrukkerije van Herdingh en Du Mortier. *Leyden, Herdingh & Du Mortier*, 1793. The Hague, 3107 B 26.   H9

556 Hakvoord, B. Algemene zend-brieven. *Amsterdam, J. Bouwer & J.* 1799 *Ratelband*, 1799. Amsterdam.   D1

557 Christelyke academie. *Turnhout, J. P. Brepols* [p. 1799]. Van Heurck 5, No. 1. Brussels.   G1

558 [Thienen, F. van.] De historie van de koninglyken propheet David. 1802 *Bruges, Widow De Moor*, 1802. Ghent, Th 4436.   B1

559 Civilité chrétienne et morale pour l'instruction des enfants et de 1804 toutes personnes . . . dressée par un missionnaire, suivi des quatrains de M. de Pibrac et d'un petit traité d'orthographe . . . le tout corrigé, augmenté et mis dans un nouvel ordre par . . . Deneufchatel. *Paris, Nyon jeune*, 1804. BN.   A2+B1

560 Jacobi, H. Gemene zendbrieven. *Venlo, Widow of H. Bontamps*, 1805. 1805 Brussels.   A4

561 Civilité honnête pour l'instruction des enfants. *Évreux, J. J. L.* 1810
Ancelle*, 1810. BN. A2+B1

562 Den nieuwen spiegel der jongheyt. *Ghent, B. Poelman*, 1810. Antwerp,
Ruusbroec; Brussels. E2a

563 La Civilité honnête. *Rouen, Mégard*, 1810. BN. A2+B1

564 La Salle, J.-B. de. Les Règles de la bienséance. *Rouen, Mégard*, 1810.
BN. A2+B1

565 La Civilité puérile et honnête. *Angers, L. Pavie*, 1811. BN. H10 1811

566 De schoone historie van de vromen en godvruchtigen jongeling
Joseph. *Ghent, J. Begyn* [1811]. Vanderhaeghen iv, 5859. Antwerp,
Ruusbroec; Brussels; Ghent. G1

567 Civilité honnête pour l'instruction des enfants. *Lens, T. Le Clère*, 1811.
BN. A2+B1

568 La Salle, J.-B. de. Les Règles de la bienséance et de la civilité chrétienne. 1812
Évreux, J. J. L. Ancelle, 1812. BN. A2+B1

569 De kleine christelyke academie, *Ghent, J. Begyn* [1812]. Antwerp, E
84155. G1

570 La Salle, J.-B. de. Les Règles de la bienséance et de la civilité chrétienne.
Paris, Montaudon, 1812. BN. A2+B1

571 La Civilité qui se pratique en France. *Angers, L. Pavie*, 1813. BN. H10 1813

572 De schoone historie van den jongeling Joseph. *Bruges, C. De Moor*,
1813. Waller 758. Antwerp, Ruusbroec; Ghent; The Hague. B1

573 La Civilité qui se pratique en France. *Poitiers, F. A. Barbier*, 1813.
BN. B2

574 La Civilité puérile et honnête. *Angers, L. Pavie*, 1814. BN. H10 1814

575 La Salle, J.-B. de. Les Règles de la bienséance. *Rouen, S. Mégard*,
1814. BN. B1

576 Den nieuwen spiegel der jongheyt of gulden ABC. *Bruges, Widow* 1815
De Moor, 1815. Antwerp, Ruusbroec. B1

577 Civilité honnête pour l'instruction des enfants. *Évreux, J. J. L. Ancelle*,
1815. BN. A2+B1

578 La Salle, J.-B. de. Les Règles de la bienséance et de la civilité chrétienne.
Paris, Montaudon, 1815. BN. A2+B1

579 La Salle, J.-B. de. Les Règles de la bienséance. *Rouen, Mégard*, 1816. 1816
BN. B1

580 Civilité honnête pour l'instruction des enfants. *Évreux, J. J. L.* 1817
Ancelle*, 1817. BN. A2+B1

581   La Salle, J.-B. de.   Les Règles de la bienséance. *St. Mâlo, L. Hovius,*
      1817. BN.   A2 + B1

582   La Salle, J.-B. de.   Les Règles de la bienséance et de la civilité chrétienne.
      Vannes, J. M. Galles, 1817. BN, R 40861.   A2 + B1

583   La Salle, J.-B. de.   Les Règles de la bienséance et de la civilité chrétienne.
      Vannes, J. M. Galles [c. 1817]. BN, R 40852.   B1

584   La Salle, J.-B. de.   Les Règles de la bienséance et de la civilité chrétienne.   1818
      Paris, J. Moronval, 1818. BN.   A2 + B1

585   La Salle, J.-B. de.   Les Règles de la bienséance et de la civilité chrétienne.   1819
      Evreux, J. J. L. Ancelle, 1819. BN.   A2 + B1

586   De kleine christelyke academie. *Ypres, L. L'Estienne* [c. 1819]. Van
      Heurck 9, No. 12. Brussels, III, 92.874 A.   E2a

587   Christelyke academie. *Louvain, Gutskoven-Franckx,* 1820. Van   1820
      Heurck 5, No. 2. Brussels.   G1

588   La Salle, J.-B. de.   Les Règles de la bienséance et de la civilité chrétienne.
      Paris, Montaudon, 1820. BN.   A2 + B1

589   [Linden, J. van der.] Heerelyke ende gelukkige reys . . . nae Jerusalem.
      Turnhout, J. Brepols [c. 1820]. Van Heurck 85, No. 112. Brussels, III,
      93.041 A.   G1

590   Civilité honnête pour l'instruction des enfants. *Évreux, J. J. L.*   1821
      Ancelle, 1821. BN.   A2 + E1

591   De schoone historie van den vroomen en godvrugtigen jongeling   1823
      Joseph. *Bruges, Widow De Moor,* 1823. Brussels; Ghent.   B1

592   La Salle, J.-B. de.   Les Règles de la bienséance et de la civilité chrétienne.
      Dijon, Douillier, 1823. BN   A2

593   La Salle, J.-B. de.   Les Règles de la bienséance et de la civilité chrétienne.
      Paris, Montaudon, 1823. BN.   A2 + B1

594   La Salle, J.-B. de.   Les Règles de la bienséance et de la civilité chrétienne.
      Vannes, J. M. Galles, 1823. BN.   A2 + B1

595   La Civilité honnête pour les enfants. *Vire, Adam,* 1823. BN. A2 + B1

596   La Salle, J.-B. de.   Les Règles de la bienséance. *Vire, Adam,* 1823. BN
                                                             A2 + B1

597   Civilité honnête pour l'instruction des enfants. *Évreux, J. J. L. Ancelle,*   1824
      1824. BN.   A2 + B1

598   La Salle, J.-B. de.   Les Règles de la bienséance et de la civilité chrétienne.
      Évreux, J. J. L. Ancelle, 1824. BN.   A2 + B1

599   La Civilité chrétienne et honnête. *Paris, J. Carez,* 1824. BN.   G1

600   Civilité honnête pour l'instruction des enfants. *Évreux, J. J. L. Ancelle,*   1825
      1825. BN.   A2+B1

601   La Salle, J.-B. de. Les Règles de la bienséance et de la civilité chrétienne.
      St. Málo, L. Hovius, 1825. BN.   A2+B1

602   La Salle, J.-B. de. Les Règles de la bienséance et de la civilité chrétienne.
      Paris, Demonville, 1825. BN.   B1

603   La Salle, J.-B. de. Les Règles de la bienséance et de la civilité chrétienne.
      Paris, J. Moronval, 1825. BN.   A2+B1

604   La Civilité chrétienne et honnête. *Toul, Bastien-Carez,* 1825. BN.   G1

605   La Salle, J.-B. de. Les Règles de la bienséance et de la civilité chrétienne.
      Vannes, J. M. Galles, 1825. BN.   A2+B1

606   La Civilité qui se pratique en France. *Poitiers, F. A. Barbier,* 1826.   1826
      BN.   B2

607   La Civilité chrétienne et honnête. *Toul, J. Carez,* 1826. BN.   G1

608   Civilité honnête pour l'instruction des enfants. *Évreux, J. J. L.*   1827
      Ancelle, 1827. BN.   A2+B1

609   Civilité honnête pour l'instruction des enfants. *Paris, J. Moronval,*
      1827. BN.   A2+B1

610   Civilité honnête pour l'instruction des enfants. *Troyes, Widow*
      André, 1827. BN.   B1

611   La Honnête civilité. *Beauvais, A. Desjardins,* 1828. BN.   A2+B1   1828

612   La Salle, J.-B. de. Les Règles de la bienséance et de la civilité chrétienne.
      Dijon, Douillier, 1828. BN.   A2

613   Civilité pour l'instruction des enfants. *Évreux, J. J. L. Ancelle,* 1829.   1829
      BN.   A2+B1

614   La Civilité chrétienne et honnête. *Toul, J. Carez,* 1829. BN.   G1

615   Civilité honnête pour l'instruction des enfants. *Paris, J. Moronval,*   1832
      1832. BN.   A2+B1

616   Civilité honnête pour l'instruction des enfants. *Paris, J. Moronval,*   1833
      1833. BN.   A2+B1

617   De schoone historie van den vromen en godvruchtigen jongeling   1834
      Joseph. *Ypres, Sauvage-Ramoen* [*c.* 1834]. Van Heurck 39, No. 46.
      Brussels, III, 92.989 A.   E2a

618   [Thienen, F. van.] De historie van den koninglyken propheet David.   1835
      Bruges, C. De Moor, 1835. Antwerp; Brussels.   B1

619   Civilité chrétienne et honnête. *Toul, Widow Bastien,* 1838. BN.   1838
                                                                        A2+B1

620   De schoone historie van ... Joseph. *Ghent, A. van der Meersch* [p.   1841
      1841]. Brussels; Ghent.   G1

621   Civilité honnête pour l'instruction des enfants. *Paris, J. Moronval,*
      1841. BN.   A2+B1

622   La Civilité chrétienne et honnête. *Toul, Widow Bastien,* 1841. BN.
                                                                       A2+B1

623   La Civilité chrétienne et honnête. *Toul, Widow Bastien,* 1842. BN.   1842
                                                                       A2+B1

624   La Civilité chrétienne et honnête. *Épinal, Pellerin,* 1843. BN. A2+B1   1843

625   La Salle, J.-B. de. Les Règles de la bienséance et de la civilité chrétienne.   1844
      Lyons, J. B. Pélagaud, 1844. BN.   A2

626   Civilité honnête pour l'instruction des enfants. *Paris, J. Moronval,*
      1844. BN.   A2+B1

627   Civilité honnête pour l'instruction des enfants. *Amiens, Caron &*   1846
      Lambert, 1846. BN.   A2+B1

628   Schmid, C. Tweede hondertal leerzame verhalen voor kinderen.   1848
      Amsterdam, Ten Brink-De Vries, 1848. Amsterdam.   D1, H1, H9

629   Schmid, C. Eerste hondertal leerzame verhalen voor kinderen. *Amster-*
      dam, Ten Brink-De Vries, 1850. Amsterdam.   D1, H1, H9

630   Civilité chrétienne et honnête. *Toul, Widow Bastien,* 1850. BN.   1850
                                                                       A2+B1

631   La Salle, J.-B. de. Les Règles de la bienséance et de la civilité chrétienne.   1851
      Edition revue par D.Pinart. *Paris, C. Fouraut,* 1851. BN.   A2+B1

632   Civilité honnête pour l'instruction des enfants. *Paris, J. Moronval,*   1857
      1857. BN.   A2+B1

633   Moll, S. Nuttig leesboek voor kinderen. *Tiel, A. van Loon,* 1857.
      Waller 1231. The Hague.   D1, H1

634   Schmid, C. Eerste honderdtal leerzame verhalen voor kinderen.   1858
      Amsterdam, Ten Brink-De Vries, 1858. Amsterdam.   D1, H1

635   La Civilité puérile et honnête. *Amiens, Caron & Lambert* [1860].   1860
      BN.   A2+B1

636   Thadeus Neapolitanus. Hystoria de desolacione et conculcatione   1874
      civitatis Acconensis. *Geneva, J. G. Tick,* 1874. BN.   A2

ADDENDA

p. 29. A partnership agreement signed by Hamon, Danfrie, and Le Royer on 18 August 1561 is printed by Mlle E. Droz in 'La Société Hamon, Danfrie & Le Royer (1561)', *Gutenberg Jahrbuch* 1965 (Mainz), pp. 43–47.

1 Quarante et neuf psalmes de David . . . traduitz . . . par C. Marot et mis en musique par Michel Ferrier. *Lyons, R. Granjon,* 1559. The Hague.   1559
A1

2 L'Histoire de l'ancien Tobie. *Antwerp, J. de Laet, c.* 1560. BM 1016. l. 9   1560
C1

3 Vargas, B. de. Breve relacion en octava rima de la jornada. *Antwerp, A. Tavernier,* 1568. Vervliet 7. Brussels.   1568
C1, 2

4 Exemplaire pour bien et proprement escrire la lettre françoise. *Paris, Nic. Bonfons,* [p. 1573]. Berlin, Staatl. Museen, Kunstbibliothek. A6, B1   1573

5 Houwaert, J. B. Pegasydes Pleyn. *Antwerp, C. Plantin,* 1583. BM; MPM.   1583
A5, A6

6 Papon, J. Instrument du premier notaire. *Lyons, J. de Tournes,* 1585. Cartier 656. Lyons.   1585
A2, A5

7 Guevara, A. de. 'T Gulden Boeck vanden loflijken Keyser . . . Marcus Aurelius. *Antwerp, A. 's Coninx,* 1586. Leyden.   1586
C2

8 Peletier, J. In Euclidis elementa geometrica demonstrationes, 2nd ed., *Lyons, J. de Tournes,* 1590. Bodl.   1590
A2, A5

9 Noot, J. van der. De poetische Werken. *Antwerp, A. 's Coninx,* 1592. MPM.   1592
A2+C1, D1

10 L'Histoire de l'ancien Tobie . . . *Lille, C. M. Cramé,* 1725. BM 3155. aa. 6   1725
E2a

11 De Kleine christelycke academie. *Ghent, Widow of M. de Goesin,* [p. 1761]. Brussels; Ghent.   1761
E3

INDEX

Upright figures refer to pages, inclined figures to items in the Appendix. Dutch ij is treated as y in the alphabetical order.

PRINTED IN GREAT BRITAIN
AT THE UNIVERSITY PRESS, OXFORD
BY VIVIAN RIDLER
PRINTER TO THE UNIVERSITY